LIBER/

William A. Galston is a distinguished political philosophic.   work is informed by his experience of having also served in public office: From 1993 to 1995 he was President Clinton's Deputy Assistant for Domestic Policy. Professor Galston is thus able to speak with an authority rare among political theorists about the implications of advancing certain moral and political values in practice.

The foundational argument of this book is that liberalism is compatible with the value pluralism first espoused by Isaiah Berlin. Professor Galston defends a version of value pluralism and argues, against the contentions of John Gray and others, that it undergirds a kind of liberal politics that gives weight to the ability of individuals and groups to live their lives in accordance with their deepest beliefs about what gives meaning and purpose to life.

Professor Galston argues against what he calls "monistic" theories of value that either reduce all goods to a common measure or create a comprehensive hierarchy among goods. He operates from very different assumptions: that value pluralism does not degenerate into relativism, that objective goods cannot be fully rank-ordered, that some goods are basic in the sense that they are key to any choiceworthy conception of life, and that there is a wide range of legitimate diversity of individual conceptions of good lives and of public cultures and purposes. From these premises William Galston explores how his liberal pluralism has important implications for political deliberation and decision making, for the design of public institutions, and for the division of legitimate authority among government, religious institutions, civil society, parents and families, and individuals.

Few contemporary writers on political theory have William Galston's status as both a significant political philosopher and political actor. This feature, combined with the nontechnical language in which the arguments are developed, should ensure that this provocative book is eagerly sought out by professionals in philosophy, political science, law, and policy making, as well as by general readers interested in these areas.

LIBERAL PLURALISM

———

The Implications of Value Pluralism for Political Theory and Practice

WILLIAM A. GALSTON

University of Maryland

CAMBRIDGE
UNIVERSITY PRESS

PUBLISHED BY THE PRESS SYNDICATE OF THE UNIVERSITY OF CAMBRIDGE
The Pitt Building, Trumpington Street, Cambridge, United Kingdom

CAMBRIDGE UNIVERSITY PRESS
The Edinburgh Building, Cambridge CB2 2RU, UK
40 West 20th Street, New York, NY 10011-4211, USA
477 Williamstown Road, Port Melbourne, VIC 3207, Australia
Ruiz de Alarcón 13, 28014 Madrid, Spain
Dock House, The Waterfront, Cape Town 8001, South Africa

http://www.cambridge.org

First published 2002

Printed in the United States of America

Typeface Sabon 10.25/13.5 pt.   *System* LATEX 2_ε [TB]

A catalog record for this book is available from the British Library.

Library of Congress Cataloging in Publication Data
Galston, William A. (William Arthur), 1946–
Liberal pluralism : the implications of value pluralism for political theory and practice /
William A. Galston.
      p.   cm.
Includes bibliographical references and index.
ISBN 0-521-81304-2 – ISBN 0-521-01249-X (pb.)
1. Liberalism.   2. Pluralism (Social sciences)   I. Title.
JC574 .G37   2002
320.51 – dc21   2001043917

ISBN 0 521 81304 2 hardback
ISBN 0 521 01249 X paperback

To the victims and heroes of September 11

Adversity doth best discover virtue.
Francis Bacon

To the victims and heroes of September 11

Adversity doth best discover virtue.
Francis Bacon

CONTENTS

ACKNOWLEDGMENTS

I am grateful to my colleagues at the University of Maryland's Institute for Philosophy and Public Policy for many years of stimulating discussions on the topics addressed in this book. I have persuaded none of them but have learned from all of them.

I have enjoyed the opportunity to present parts of my arguments at meetings organized by the IIT Chicago-Kent College of Law, the College of William and Mary School of Law, the University of Maryland School of Law, the Philosophy Department of George Washington University, the Political Science Department of the University of Chicago, the Social Philosophy and Policy Center of Bowling Green State University, the American Society for Political and Legal Philosophy, and the Institute for Political Studies of the Portuguese Catholic University. The dialogue on those occasions contributed significantly to the development of this book.

Earlier versions of portions of this book have appeared in the *American Political Science Review*, the *William and Mary Law Review*, and *Ethics*, and in *Democracy*, edited by Ellen Frankel Paul, Fred D. Miller, Jr., and Jeffrey Paul (Cambridge University Press, 2000). I am grateful for the necessary permissions to make use of these materials in revised form.

I also wish to acknowledge the recent publication of two important works that deal with some of the topics I take up in this book: Andrew Mason's *Community, Solidarity, and Belonging: Levels of Community and Their Normative Significance* (Cambridge University Press, 2000) and Jeff Spinner-Halev's *Surviving Diversity: Religion and Democratic Citizenship* (Johns Hopkins University Press, 2000). I regret that these books came to my attention too late to allow me at this time to address the significant arguments they present. I hereby offer these authors (and others I may have neglected) a promissory note for the future.

LIBERAL PLURALISM

PART I

——

INTRODUCTION

PLURALISM IN ETHICS
AND POLITICS

This book brings together and develops themes that have occupied me over the past decade of scholarly and public life. It defends a liberal theory of politics that is pluralist rather than monist and (in John Rawls's sense) comprehensive rather than freestanding or "political."

LIBERALISM

Let me begin by stating what I believe it means to be a liberal, in the theoretical, not political, sense of the term.

Liberalism requires a robust though rebuttable presumption in favor of individuals and groups leading their lives as they see fit, within a broad range of legitimate variation, in accordance with their own understanding of what gives life meaning and value. I call this presumption the principle of *expressive liberty.* This principle implies a corresponding presumption (also rebuttable) against external interference with individual and group endeavors.

To create a secure space within which individuals and groups may lead their lives, public institutions are needed. Liberal public institutions may restrict the activities of individuals and groups for four kinds of reasons: first, to reduce coordination problems and conflict among diverse legitimate activities and to adjudicate such conflict when it cannot be avoided; second, to prevent and when necessary punish transgressions individuals may commit against one another; third, to guard the boundary separating legitimate from illegitimate variations among ways of life; and finally, to secure the conditions – including cultural and civic conditions – needed to sustain public institutions over time. Specifying the content of these conditions requires a mode of inquiry that is empirical as well as theoretical.

Two consequences follow from this account of public institutions. First, for public purposes, the value of these institutions, and of the public activities they shape, is understood as instrumental rather than intrinsic. For some individuals, to be sure, public life will be an element (perhaps even the dominant element) of what they define as the intrinsic meaning and value of their own lives, but this conception is not part of an understanding of liberal politics that is binding on all members of the political community. An instrumental rather than intrinsic account of the worth of politics forms a key distinction between liberalism and civic republicanism.

Second, liberal public institutions are understood as limited rather than plenipotentiary. There are multiple, independent, sometimes competing sources of authority over our lives, and political authority is not dominant for all purposes under all circumstances. Liberalism accepts the importance of political institutions but refuses to regard them as architectonic. (I call this understanding of the limits of politics the principle of *political pluralism*.)

If this is roughly what liberalism means, why be a liberal? One answer draws from experience and common sense: Broadly liberal public regimes tend over time to satisfy more of the legitimate needs of their publics and to generate more unforced, sustained loyalty than do other forms of political association. A second answer (offered by John Rawls in *Political Liberalism*)[1] suggests that liberalism draws from, and comports with, a widely shared stock of freestanding moral premises concerning relations among human beings and the nature of political association.

PLURALISM AND MONISM

While each of these answers has merit, neither is sufficient. I suggest that liberalism derives much of its power from its consistency with the account of the moral world offered by Isaiah Berlin and known as value pluralism. The concluding section of Berlin's "Two Concepts of

---

1 John Rawls, *Political Liberalism; with a New Introduction and the "Reply to Habermas"* (New York: Columbia University Press, 1996).

Liberty"[2] has helped spark what may now be regarded as a full-fledged value-pluralist movement in contemporary moral philosophy. Leading contributors to this movement include Bernard Williams, Stuart Hampshire, Joseph Raz, Steven Lukes, Michael Stocker, Thomas Nagel, Charles Taylor, Martha Nussbaum, Charles Larmore, John Gray, and John Kekes.[3] During the past decade, moral philosophers have clarified and debated many of the complex technical issues raised by value pluralism, as well as broader objections to the overall approach.[4]

Throughout this book I explore many of these issues and defend value pluralism at some length. For the purposes of this introduction, a few basics will suffice.

1. Value pluralism is not relativism. The distinction between good and bad, and between good and evil, is objective and rationally defensible.

2. Objective goods cannot be fully rank-ordered. This means that there is no common measure for all goods, which are qualitatively heterogeneous. It means that there is no summum bonum that is the chief good for all individuals. It means that there are no comprehensive lexical orderings among types of goods. It also means that there is no "first virtue of social institutions"[5] but, rather, a range of public goods and virtues the relative importance of which will depend on circumstances.

2 In Isaiah Berlin, *Four Essays on Liberty* (Oxford: Oxford University Press, 1969).

3 See Bernard Williams, "Conflicts of Values," in *Moral Luck* (Cambridge: Cambridge University Press, 1981); Stuart Hampshire, "Morality and Conflict," in *Morality and Conflict* (Cambridge, Mass.: Harvard University Press, 1983); Joseph Raz, *The Morality of Freedom* (Oxford: Clarendon Press, 1986); Steven Lukes, "Making Sense of Moral Conflict," in *Moral Conflict and Politics* (Oxford: Clarendon Press, 1991); Michael Stocker, *Plural and Conflicting Values* (Oxford: Clarendon Press, 1990); Thomas Nagel, "The Fragmentation of Value," in *Mortal Questions* (Cambridge: Cambridge University Press, 1979); Charles Taylor, "The Diversity of Goods," in Amartya Sen and Bernard Williams, eds., *Utilitarianism and Beyond* (Cambridge: Cambridge University Press, 1982); Martha Nussbaum, *The Fragility of Goodness: Luck and Ethics in Greek Tragedy and Philosophy* (Cambridge: Cambridge University Press, 1986); Charles Larmore, *Patterns of Moral Complexity* (Cambridge: Cambridge University Press, 1987); John Gray, *Isaiah Berlin* (Princeton, N.J.: Princeton University Press, 1996); John Kekes, *The Morality of Pluralism* (Princeton, N.J.: Princeton University Press, 1993).

4 See Ruth Chang, ed., *Incommensurability, Incomparability, and Practical Reason* (Cambridge, Mass.: Harvard University Press, 1997); also Glen Newey, "Metaphysics Postponed: Liberalism, Pluralism, and Neutrality," *Political Studies* 45 (1997): 296–311, and "Value Pluralism in Contemporary Liberalism," *Dialogue* 37 (1998): 493–522.

5 Which John Rawls asserts justice to be in *A Theory of Justice* (Cambridge, Mass.: Harvard University Press, 1971).

3. Some goods are basic in the sense that they form part of any choiceworthy conception of a human life. To be deprived of such goods is to be forced to endure the great evils of existence. All decent regimes endeavor to minimize the frequency and scope of such deprivations.

4. Beyond this parsimonious list of basic goods, there is a wide range of legitimate diversity – of individual conceptions of good lives, and also of public cultures and public purposes. This range of legitimate diversity defines the zone of individual liberty, and also of deliberation and democratic decision making. Where necessity (natural or moral) ends, choice begins.

5. Value pluralism is distinguished from various forms of what I will call "monism." A theory of value is monistic, I will say, if it either (a) reduces goods to a common measure or (b) creates a comprehensive hierarchy or ordering among goods.

Just as one must ask why it makes sense to be a liberal, one must ask why value pluralism is to be preferred to the various forms of monism that thinkers have advanced since the beginning of philosophy as we know it. In the course of this book I shall try to develop a systematic answer, but a few preliminary remarks may be helpful.

To begin, monistic accounts of value lead to procrustean distortions of moral argument. The vicissitudes of hedonism and utilitarianism in this respect are well known. Even Kant could not maintain the position that the good will is the only good with moral weight; whence his account of the "highest good," understood as a heterogeneous composite of inner worthiness and external good fortune.

Second, our moral experience suggests that the tension among broad structures or theories of value – consequentialism, deontology, and virtue theory; general and particular obligations; regard for others and justified self-regard – is rooted in a genuine heterogeneity (or as Thomas Nagel puts it, "fragmentation") of value. If so, no amount of philosophical argument or cultural progress can lead to the definitive victory of one account of value over the rest. Moral reflection is the effort to bring different dimensions of value to bear on specific occasions of judgment and to determine how they are best balanced or ordered, given the facts of the case.

Similar difficulties arise when we are confronted with a plurality of specific interests or goods, rather than of moral structures. For some years I served as a White House official responsible for managing a portion of domestic policy on behalf of the president. Over and over again I had the same experience: I would be chairing an interagency task force designed to reach a unified administration position on some legislative or regulatory proposal. As the representatives of the departments argued for their various views, I found it impossible to dismiss any one of them as irrelevant to the decision, or as wholly lacking in weight. Nor could I reduce the competing considerations to a common measure of value; so far as I or anyone else could tell, they were irreducibly heterogeneous. The issues were qualitative, not quantitative: In the particular circumstances, which considerations should be regarded as more important, or more urgent? If a balance was to be struck, what weighting of competing goods could reasonably be regarded as fair?

I found it remarkable how often we could reach deliberative closure in the face of this heterogeneity. Many practitioners (and not a few philosophers) shy away from value pluralism out of fear that it leads to deliberative anarchy. Experience suggests that this is not necessarily so. There can be right answers, widely recognized as such, even in the absence of general rules for ordering or aggregating diverse goods.

It is true, as John Rawls pointed out more than thirty years ago, that pluralism on the level of values does not rule out, in principle, the existence of general rules for attaching weights to particular values or of establishing at least a partial ordering among them.[6] But in practice, these rules prove vulnerable to counterexamples or extreme situations. As Brian Barry observes, Rawls's own effort to establish lexical priorities among heterogeneous goods does not succeed: "[S]uch a degree of simplicity is not to be obtained. We shall . . . have to accept the unavoidability of balancing, and we shall also have to accept a greater variety of principles than Rawls made room for."[7] But, to repeat, the moral particularism I am urging is compatible with the existence of right answers in specific cases; there may be compelling reasons to conclude that certain trade-offs among competing goods are preferable to others.

---

6 See John Rawls, *A Theory of Justice*, p. 42.

7 Brian Barry, *Political Argument; A Reissue with a New Introduction* (Berkeley: University of California Press, 1990), p. lxxi. Barry goes on to suggest that something like the Original Position, understood as embodying the requirement that valid principles must be capable of receiving the free assent of all those affected by them, might nonetheless lead to general principles for balancing competing values.

COMPREHENSIVE AND FREESTANDING
POLITICAL THEORIES

Some philosophers argue that it is theoretically improper and practically imprudent to link political principles to other parts of philosophy, even ethics or value theory. Political theory should be freestanding, not "comprehensive." For reasons that I discuss at length in Chapter 4, I disagree: Political theory cannot be walled off from our general understanding of what is good and valuable for human beings, or from our understanding of how human existence is linked to other beings and to existence simpliciter. I am not advocating "foundationalism"; indeed, it is not clear that this architectural metaphor really clarifies anything. The point is not foundations but, rather, connections. Theories in any given domain of inquiry typically point to propositions whose validity is explored in other domains. Thought crosses boundaries.[8]

FOUR TYPES OF POLITICAL THEORY

On the basis of the twin distinctions between pluralism and monism and between comprehensive and freestanding conceptions, I suggest that there are four main types of political theory:

1. *freestanding/monist*. John Rawls's *Political Liberalism* is an example; it seeks to decouple political theory from other domains of inquiry while preserving the various lexical orderings defended in *A Theory of Justice*.

2. *comprehensive/monist*. Classical utilitarianism is an example of this kind of theory. So, intriguingly, is Ronald Dworkin's latest contribution.[9]

3. *freestanding/pluralist*. Michael Walzer's *Spheres of Justice* is an example of this category. While Walzer offers a wide range of legitimate plural values both among and within public cultures and refuses to give any public value pride of place for all purposes, he proceeds empirically/historically and refrains from proposing any broader theory of good, value, or existence.

---

8 See my *Liberal Purposes* (Cambridge: Cambridge University Press, 1991), Chapter 2.

9 See his *Sovereign Virtue: The Theory and Practice of Equality* (Cambridge, Mass.: Harvard University Press, 2000), pp. 4–5. For a fuller account, see my review in *The Review of Politics* 63, 3 (Summer 2001): 607–611.

4. *comprehensive/pluralist.* On some interpretations, Joseph Raz's *Morality of Freedom* is an example of this genre. In recent writings, John Gray uses comprehensive pluralism to argue for a vision of politics in which institutional and deliberative legitimacy reflects a wide range of local conditions.

In this book, I present and defend what I call "liberal pluralism" as the preferred conception of comprehensive/pluralist theory. In the process, I argue against taking autonomy to be a defining liberal value, as Raz appears to do, and also against Gray's effort to drive a wedge between pluralism and liberalism.

THE CONSEQUENCES OF PLURALISM

The consequences of pluralism include not only a distinctive type of political theory but also distinctive conceptions of (inter alia) public culture, public philosophy, constitutionalism, deliberation, public policy, democracy, and free association. For example, from a liberal pluralist point of view, I argue, there are multiple types of legitimate decision making, and democracy is not trumps for all purposes. Another example: From a liberal pluralist point of view, public institutions must be cautious and restrained in their dealings with voluntary associations, and there is no presumption that a state may intervene in such associations just because they conduct their internal affairs in ways that diverge from general public principles.

The relationship between voluntary associations and publicly enforced civic norms has emerged as a key point of disagreement among contemporary liberals. Some argue that civic goods are important, or fragile, enough to warrant substantial state interference with civil associations. It is a mistake, they believe, to give anything like systematic deference to associational claims.[10] I disagree. I begin with the intuition that free association yields important human goods and that the state bears a burden of proof whenever it seeks to intervene. My accounts

---

10 Two important recent examples of this genre are Stephen Macedo, *Diversity and Distrust: Civic Education in a Multicultural Democracy* (Cambridge, Mass.: Harvard University Press, 2000), and Brian Barry, *Culture and Equality* (Cambridge, Mass.: Harvard University Press, 2001). For remarks on Macedo, see my review in *Ethics* 112, 2 (January 2002): 386–391. For Barry, see my review in *The Public Interest* 144 (Summer 2001): 100–108.

of value pluralism, expressive liberty, and political pluralism lend theoretical support to this intuition and help explain why we should not see state power as plenipotentiary.

PLURALISM AND CIVIC UNITY

While focused on individual and associational liberty, the account of politics I offer in this book is certainly not anarchist, libertarian, or even "classical-liberal." I make a place for citizenship and civic virtue and for education directed toward their cultivation. Some readers may believe that on its face, this civic dimension of my argument is at odds with my pluralist professions.

I think not. Pluralism does not abolish civic unity. Rather, it leads to a distinctive understanding of the relation between the requirements of unity and the claims of diversity in liberal politics. Liberty cannot be exercised or sustained without a public system of liberty. Politics may be instrumentally rather than intrinsically good, and partial rather than plenipotentiary, but it is nonetheless essential. There is no invisible civic hand that sustains a system of liberty; such a system must be consciously reproduced. There are limits that education conducted or required by a liberal pluralist state must not breach. But within those bounds it is legitimate and necessary and must be robust.

THE PLAN OF THIS BOOK

The argument of this book proceeds as follows:

Beginning with a puzzle about the relation between civic unity and associational plurality, Chapter 2 distinguishes between two approaches to liberalism – one based on the core value of individual rational autonomy, the other on respect for legitimate difference – and argues for the diversity-based approach as offering a better chance for individuals and groups to live their lives in accordance with their distinctive conceptions of what gives meaning and value to life. Chapter 3 begins the task of defending this preference by offering three sources of legitimate diversity: expressive liberty understood as the fit between outward existence and inner conceptions of value; Berlinian value pluralism; and political pluralism understood, along the lines of early-twentieth-century British thinkers such as Figgis, as the denial of the plenipotentiary power of state institutions over all aspects of social life. Chapter 4 defends the propriety of linking political theory to other branches of philosophy (especially moral theory) by questioning the cogency of Rawls's rejection of "comprehensive" theorizing. Chapter 5 argues, against John Gray and others, that Berlin was right to see deep compatibility – relations of mutual support – between value pluralism and liberal politics. Exploring an analogy with jurisprudence, Chapter 6 offers an account of presumptions as a way of moving from open-ended value pluralism to the kinds of partial agreements that organized political life requires.

Chapter 7 argues that if we take value pluralism seriously, we are driven to understand democracy as only one among several legitimate sources of political authority and modes of decision making. Chapter 8 suggests that if we follow through the implications of the three sources of legitimate diversity discussed in Chapter 3, we must conclude that the authority of state institutions over the education of children, while robust, is nonetheless limited by parental claims that are morally fundamental, rather than derivative from contingent public decisions. Chapter 9 brings many of these considerations together into an account of the public framework and constitutional principles of the liberal pluralist state. Chapter 10 concludes the argument with reflections on the relation between value pluralism and key civic goals of justice and unity.

PART II

FROM VALUE
PLURALISM TO LIBERAL
PLURALIST THEORY

2

TWO CONCEPTS
OF LIBERALISM

THE CIVIC AND EXPRESSIVE DIMENSIONS
OF LIBERALISM

Above and beyond artful institutional contrivances, liberal democracies rely on cultural and moral conditions that cannot be taken for granted. But to remain "liberal," these regimes must safeguard a sphere in which individuals and groups can act, without state interference, in ways that reflect their understanding of what gives meaning and value to their lives. What is the relationship between the "civic" and the "expressive" strands of liberalism? What should we do when state action designed to bolster the preconditions of liberal democracy constrains expressive liberty in troubling ways, or conversely, when the exercise of expressive liberty is at odds with what may be regarded as liberal democratic preconditions? This conflict inevitably arises in public institutions, such as schools. But it also emerges when the state seeks to regulate the structure and conduct of voluntary associations.

Must civil associations mirror the constitutional order if they are to sustain that order? The resolution of this issue revolves in part around empirical questions: For example, to what extent do illiberal or undemocratic voluntary associations engender patterns of conduct, belief, and character that weaken liberal democratic polities? There is no agreement among scholars on this point, certainly not in general, and rarely in specific cases. Theorists such as Stephen Macedo are right to emphasize the dangers of complacency. Liberal democratic citizens are made, not born, and we cannot blithely rely on the invisible hand of civil society to carry out civic paideia.[1]

[1] Macedo, "Transformative Constitutionalism and the Case of Religion: Defending the Moderate Hegemony of Liberalism," *Political Theory* 26, 1 (February 1998): 56–80.

On the other hand, Nancy Rosenblum has urged attention to the dynamics of moral and political psychology; theoretical abstractions can lead us to overestimate the actual importance of "congruence" between regime-level principles and the associations of civil society.[2] Incongruity evokes fears that frequently outrun facts, as they did in the nineteenth century when waves of Catholic immigration led Protestant Americans to worry about the future of democratic institutions. Notwithstanding these fears, Catholics soon became the most loyal of citizens – and among the most adept at the game of grassroots democratic politics.

Rosenblum asks us to look at different functions of civil associations. They can express liberty as well as personal or social identity; provide arenas for the accommodation of deep differences; temper individual self-interest; help integrate otherwise disconnected individuals into society; nurture trust; serve as seedbeds of citizenship; and resist the totalizing tendencies of both closed communities and state power.[3]

It is not obvious as an empirical matter that civil society organizations within liberal democracies must be organized along liberal democratic lines in order to perform some or all of these functions. Many of the fears Protestants voiced a century ago about the antidemocratic tendencies of Catholicism are now being redirected toward Protestant fundamentalism. But it appears that in practice, these denominations, far from undermining democracy, are serving as arenas of political mobilization and education. Consider recent findings reported by the political scientists Sidney Verba, Kay Schlozman, and Henry Brady: These churches serve as important training grounds for political skills, particularly for those without large amounts of other politically relevant assets, such as education and money.[4]

There is room for deep disagreement about the policies that many religious groups are advocating in the political arena. But there seems little doubt that these groups have fostered political education and engagement to an extent few other kinds of associations can match, at a time when most social forces are pushing toward political and civic

---

2 Rosenblum, "Civil Societies: Liberalism and the Moral Uses of Pluralism," *Social Research* 61, 3 (Fall 1994): 539–562.
3 Ibid.
4 Sidney Verba, Kay Lehman Schlozman, and Henry E. Brady, *Voice and Equality: Civic Volunteerism in American Politics* (Cambridge, Mass.: Harvard University Press, 1995).

disengagement. And they seem to have done so without undermining their members' commitment to democratic pluralism. Alan Wolfe's recent empirical study of middle-class morality shows that among self-declared religious conservatives, support for core democratic principles and for tolerance of difference is very high.[5]

While the impact of civil society on the formation of citizens is a legitimate concern, the burden of proof lies with those who seek to shape or restrict the internal life of nonpublic associations. In my judgment, the available evidence does not warrant alarm, certainly not to the point of justifying new intrusions into parental and associational practices.

The empirical relation between the civic and expressive dimensions of liberal democracy is nested in a conceptual issue: What is the content of the citizenship that institutions should be trying to strengthen? Without venturing a precise answer, let me offer a general hypothesis: The more demanding the conception of citizenship, the more intrusive the public policies needed to promote it. Toward the beginning of the *Emile,* Rousseau retells Plutarch's story of the Spartan mother with five sons in the army. A Helot arrives with the news that all have been slain in battle. "Vile slave," she retorts, "was that what I asked you?" "We have won the victory," he replied, whereupon the Spartan mother hastened to the temple to give thanks to the gods. Rousseau comments laconically: That was a citizen. The example may seem far-fetched, but the point is clear: The more our conception of the good citizen requires the sacrifice of private attachments to the common good, the more vigorously the state must act (as Sparta did) to weaken those attachments in favor of devotion to the public sphere. (This point applies, mutatis mutandis, to other demanding concepts of citizenship based on ideals such as autonomy, critical rationality, and deliberative excellence.)

Within the civic republican tradition, state intrusion to foster good citizens poses no threshold issues; not so for liberal democracy, whose core commitments place limits on the measures the state may legitimately employ. I want to explore the resources liberal theory can bring to bear on the adjudication of these tensions, taking as my point of departure some examples from U.S. constitutional law.

---

5 Wolfe, *One Nation, After All* (New York: Viking, 1998), especially Chapters 2 and 3.

CIVIC AND EXPRESSIVE DIMENSIONS
OF AMERICAN CONSTITUTIONALISM

Reflecting the nativist passions stirred by World War I, the state of Nebraska passed a law forbidding instruction in any modern language other than English. A teacher in a Lutheran parochial school was convicted under this statute for the crime of teaching a Bible class in German. In *Meyer v. Nebraska,* decided in 1923, the Supreme Court struck down this law as a violation of the liberty guarantee of the Fourteenth Amendment. Writing for the court, Justice McReynolds declared:

That the State may do much, go very far, indeed, in order to improve the quality of its citizens, physically, mentally, and morally, is clear; but the individual has certain fundamental rights which must be respected. . . . The desire of the legislature to foster a homogeneous people with American ideas prepared readily to understand current discussions of civic matters is easy to appreciate. . . . But the means adopted, we think, exceed the limitations upon the power of the State and conflict with rights assured to plaintiff.[6]

The majority decision identified the underlying theory of the Nebraska law with the plenipotentiary state of Sparta, as well as with Plato's *Republic,* which it quoted at length and sharply distinguished from the underlying premises of liberal constitutionalism.

Consider, second, *Pierce v. Society of Sisters,* decided in 1925.[7] Through a ballot initiative, the people of Oregon had adopted a law requiring parents and legal guardians to send all students between the ages of eight and sixteen to public schools. The Society of Sisters, an Oregon corporation that among other activities maintained a system of Catholic schools, sued to overturn this law as inconsistent with the Fourteenth Amendment. The Supreme Court emphatically agreed:

The fundamental theory of liberty upon which all governments in this Union repose excludes any general power of the State to standardize its children by forcing them to accept instruction from public teachers only. The child is not the mere creature of the State; those who nurture him and direct his destiny have the right, coupled with the high duty, to recognize and prepare him for additional obligations.[8]

6 262 U.S. 401, 402.
7 268 U.S. 510.
8 268 U.S. 535. I agree with Macedo that we should not oversimplify the holding of these cases to create parental or associational rights that always trump civic concerns. The

Consider, finally, the case of *Wisconsin v. Yoder*, decided by the Supreme Court a quarter century ago.[9] This case presented a clash between a Wisconsin state law, which required school attendance until age sixteen, and the Old Order Amish, who claimed that high school attendance would undermine their faith-based community life. The majority of the Court agreed with the Amish and denied that the state of Wisconsin had made a compelling case for intervening against their practices: "[H]owever strong the State's interest in universal compulsory education, it is by no means absolute to the exclusion or subordination of all other interests.... [T]his case involves the fundamental interest of parents, as contrasted with that of the State, to guide the religious future and education of their children."[10]

Taken together, these cases stand for two propositions. First, in a liberal democracy, there is in principle a division of authority between parents and the state. The state has the right to establish certain minimum standards, such as the duty of parents to educate their children, and to specify some minimum content of that education, wherever it may be conducted. But parents have a wide and protected range of choices as to how the duty to educate is to be discharged. Suitably revised and extended, these considerations apply to the liberties of civil associations as well. Second, there are some things the liberal state may not do, *even in the name of forming good citizens.* The appeal to the requisites of civic education is powerful, but not always dispositive when opposed by claims based on the authority of parents or the liberties of individuals and associations.

A free society, these cases suggest, will defend the liberty of individuals to lead many different ways of life. It will protect a zone within which individuals will freely associate to pursue shared purposes and express distinctive identities. It will adhere to what lawyers would call a rebuttable presumption in favor of liberty: The burden of proof lies with those who seek to restrict associational liberty, not those who defend it.

point (and the language of the opinions makes this clear) is that neither such rights nor the civic domain enjoys a generalized priority over the other. Rather, they are independent claims, the conflicts among which must be adjudicated with regard to the structure of specific situations. See Stephen Macedo, *Diversity and Distrust: Civic Education in a Multicultural Democracy* (Cambridge, Mass.: Harvard University Press, 2000), Chapter 3.

9 406 U.S. 205 (1972).
10 406 U.S. 215, 232.

During the twentieth century, the extension of state power has multiplied the public principles held to be binding on families and civil associations. Many of these principles are designed to ensure that these associations do not arbitrarily exclude, or abuse, specific individuals; they promote public purposes widely accepted as morally compelling.

We are familiar with the moral advantages of central state power; we must also attend to its moral costs. There is what might be called a paradox of diversity: If we insist that each civil association mirror the principles of the overarching political community, then meaningful differences among associations all but disappear; constitutional uniformity crushes social pluralism. If, as I shall argue, our moral world contains plural and conflicting values, then the overzealous enforcement of general public principles runs the risk of interfering with morally legitimate individual and associational practices.

My argument constitutes a challenge both to the classical Greek conception of the political order as the all-encompassing association and to the Hobbesian/Austinian/Weberian conception of plenipotentiary sovereign power. A liberal polity guided (as I believe it should be) by a commitment to moral and political pluralism will be parsimonious in specifying binding public principles and cautious about employing such principles to intervene in the internal affairs of civil associations. It will, rather, pursue a policy of *maximum feasible accommodation,* limited only by the core requirements of individual security and civic unity.

That there are costs to such a policy cannot reasonably be denied. It will permit internal associational practices (for example, patriarchal gender relations) of which many strongly disapprove. It will allow many associations to define their membership in ways that may be seen as restraints on individual liberty. And it will, within limits, protect those whose words and way of life express deep disagreement with the regime in which they live. But unless liberty – individual and associational – is to be narrowed dramatically, these costs must be accepted.

DIVERSITY RATHER THAN AUTONOMY

The tension between the advocates of civic liberalism and the defenders of individual and associational liberty is rooted in two quite different variants of liberal thought based on two distinct principles, which I shall summarize under the headings of autonomy and diversity.

By "autonomy" I mean individual self-direction in at least one of many senses explored by John Locke, Immanuel Kant, John Stuart Mill, and Americans writing in an Emersonian vein. Liberal autonomy is frequently linked with the commitment to sustained rational examination of self, others, and social practices – whence Mill's invocation of Socrates as liberal hero. By "diversity" I mean, straightforwardly, legitimate differences among individuals and groups over such matters as the nature of the good life, sources of moral authority, reason versus faith, and the like.

A standard liberal view (or hope) is that autonomy and diversity fit together and complement one another: The exercise of autonomy yields diversity, while the fact of diversity protects and nourishes autonomy. By contrast, my less optimistic view is that these principles do not always, or usually, cohere; that in practice, they point in quite different directions in such currently disputed areas as education, rights of association, and the free exercise of religion. Indeed, many such disputes can be understood as a conflict between these two principles. Specifically, the decision to throw state power behind the promotion of individual autonomy can undermine the lives of individuals and groups that do not and cannot organize their affairs in accordance with that principle without undermining the deepest sources of their identity.

In this connection, the failure of the most systematic recent effort to harmonize group diversity and individual autonomy is instructive. In his book *Liberalism, Community, and Culture*,[11] Will Kymlicka argues that protection of minority cultures is not only consistent with, but actually required for, the promotion of individual autonomy, because such cultures constitute the environment within which many individual are able to make meaningful choices. But there is an obvious problem: Many cultures or groups do not place a high value on choice and (to say the least) do not encourage their members to exercise it. As Chandran Kukathas has argued in a searching critique of Kymlicka's thesis, if choice and critical reflection are the dominant public values, then society will be drawn down the path of interfering with groups that do not accept these values: "By insisting that the cultural community place a high value on individual choice, the larger society would in effect be saying that the minority culture must become much more liberal."[12]

11 Will Kymlicka, *Liberalism, Community, and Culture* (Oxford: Oxford University Press, 1989).
12 Chandran Kukathas, "Are There Any Cultural Rights?" *Political Theory* 20, 1 (February 1992): 122.

Kymlicka concedes the problem, if not quite the conundrum. As he says, "Finding a way to liberalize a cultural community without destroying it is a task that liberals face in every country, once we recognize the importance of a secure cultural context of choice."[13] The difficulty with this, as I have already suggested, is that what Kymlicka calls liberalization will in many cases amount to a forced shift of basic group identity; it turns out to be the cultural equivalent of the Vietnam-era principle of destroying the village in order to save it.

In the face of this conflict, many contemporary political theorists and students of jurisprudence have forthrightly given pride of place to autonomy over diversity. According to Don Herzog, "Parents need to teach their children to be critical thinkers.... Children taught the skills of questioning their own commitments are better off. They can sculpt their own identities."[14] For Stephen Macedo:

Liberal persons are distinguished by the possession of self-governing reflective capacities. Further developing these reflective capacities leads one toward the ideal of autonomy.... Striving for autonomy involves developing the self-conscious, self-critical, reflective capacities that allow one to formulate, evaluate, and revise ideals of life and character, to bring these evaluations to bear on actual choices and on the formulation of projects and commitments.[15]

Taking as his point of departure Salman Rushdie's defense of *The Satanic Verses* against the Ayatollah Khomeini's fatwa, Jeremy Waldron has developed a conception of cosmopolitan liberalism opposed in principle to confining particularism. The passage from Rushdie that most inspires Waldron runs as follows:

Those who oppose [this book] most vociferously today are of the opinion that intermingling with a different culture will inevitably weaken and ruin their own. I am of the opposite opinion. *The Satanic Verses* celebrates hybridity, impurity, intermingling, the transformation that comes of new and unexpected combinations of human beings, cultures, ideas, politics, movies, songs. It rejoices in mongrelization and fears the absolutism of the Pure.[16]

13 Kymlicka, *Liberalism, Community, and Culture*, p. 170.
14 *Happy Slaves: A Critique of Consent Theory* (Chicago: University of Chicago Press, 1989), p. 242.
15 *Liberal Virtues: Citizenship, Virtue, and Community in Liberal Constitutionalism* (Oxford: Clarendon Press, 1990), p. 269.
16 Quoted in Waldron, "Multiculturalism and Mélange," in Robert K. Fullinwider, ed., *Public Education in a Multicultural Society: Policy, Theory, Critique* (Cambridge: Cambridge University Press, 1996), p. 105.

My objection to all these views is more or less the same: Properly understood, liberalism is about the protection of legitimate diversity. A liberal state need not and should not take sides on such issues as purity versus mixture or reason versus tradition. To place an ideal of autonomous choice – let alone cosmopolitan bricolage – at the core of liberalism is in fact to narrow the range of possibilities available within liberal societies. In the guise of protecting the capacity for diversity, the autonomy principle in fact exerts a kind of homogenizing pressure on ways of life that do not embrace autonomy. In this respect, though not others, I agree with Charles Larmore when he asserts that "[t]he Kantian and Millian conceptions of liberalism [which rest on autonomy and individuality as specifications of the good life] are not adequate solutions to the political problem of reasonable disagreement about the good life. They have themselves simply become another part of the problem."[17]

What we need instead is an understanding of liberalism that gives diversity its due. This understanding is expressed in public principles, institutions, and practices that afford maximum feasible space for the enactment of individual and group differences, constrained only by the ineliminable requirements of liberal social unity.

To avoid misunderstanding, I should say that these requirements are more than minimal. The liberal state cannot be understood as comprehensively neutral. Rather, it is properly characterized as a community organized in pursuit of a distinctive ensemble of public purposes. It is these purposes that undergird its unity, structure its institutions, guide its policies, and define its public virtues. In the constitutional context, it is these purposes that shape an appropriate understanding of compelling state interests that warrant public interference with group practices.[18] Let me offer three examples:

1. A central liberal purpose – the protection of human life – would allow the liberal state to intervene against religious worship that involves human sacrifice: no free exercise for Aztecs.

2. Another central liberal purpose – the protection and promotion of normal development of basic capacities – would allow the state to intervene against communities that bind infants' skulls or malnourish them in ways that impede physical growth and maturation.

17 Larmore, "Political Liberalism," *Political Theory* 18, 3 (August 1990): 345.
18 William A. Galston, *Liberal Purposes: Goods, Virtues, and Diversity in the Liberal State* (Cambridge: Cambridge University Press, 1991), Introduction.

3. A third liberal purpose – the development of what I call "social rationality" (the kind of understanding needed to participate in the society, economy, and polity) – would allow the state to intervene against forms of education that are systematically disenabling when judged against this norm.

The point, to which I shall return, is that we cannot give diversity its due without attending to its institutional preconditions. Still, beyond the unity required for and provided by shared liberal purposes, the liberal state must allow the fullest possible scope for diversity. And the promotion of personal autonomy, understood as choice based on critical rationalism, is not among the shared liberal purposes. Autonomy is one possible mode of existence in liberal societies – one among many others. Its practice must be respected and safeguarded, but the devotees of autonomy must recognize the need for respectful coexistence with individuals and groups that do not give autonomy pride of place.

HISTORICAL ROOTS OF THE DISPUTE

Thus far I have presented autonomy and diversity as competing theoretical conceptions and moral commitments. I now want to add a further layer to the discussion. The clash between autonomy and diversity is not accidental, nor is it simply a feature of contemporary theory and practice. Rather, it is deeply rooted in the historical development of liberalism.

Liberal autonomy, I shall argue, is linked to an historical impulse often associated with the Enlightenment – namely, liberation through reason from externally imposed authority. Within this context, reason is understood as the prime source of authority; the examined life is understood as superior to reliance on tradition or faith; preference is given to self-direction over external determination; and appropriate relationships to conceptions of good or of value, and especially conceptions that constitute groups, are held to originate only through acts of conscious individual reflection on and commitment to such conceptions.

Liberal diversity, by contrast, is linked to what I shall call the post-Reformation project – that is, to the effort to deal with the political consequences of religious differences in the wake of divisions within

24

Christendom.[19] This effort gave rise to a number of competing strategies, principally the following:

First was the overcoming of differences through separation into smaller, homogeneous political units. The problem is now (and was then) that in communities of any significant size, homogeneity can never be fully achieved. As the former Yugoslav republics are discovering, the separationist impulse yields a logic of endless subdivision.

Second was restoration of homogeneity through coercive imposition. This was the preferred solution of Thomas Hobbes, and also of the young John Locke, which he later rejected on the grounds that it exacerbated the conflicts it was meant to resolve.

Third was the restoration of homogeneity through rationalization of tradition-encrusted religious particularities into a single religion of reason. This was the hope of Spinoza, and also of Thomas Jefferson, who once declared his conviction that the generation of young Americans after his own would surely all be Unitarians. This represents the clearest point of tangency between the Enlightenment impulse and the Reformation project; the only problem is that contrary to the hopes of Spinoza and Jefferson, it doesn't work that way in practice.

The final strategy, which proved most decisive for the development of liberalism, was that of accepting and managing diversity through mutual "toleration." Within a framework of civic unity, a plurality of religions could be allowed to coexist. It was in fact this religious diversity that undergirds, and eventually sets in motion the development of, our wider conception of individual and cultural differences. And thus, any reasonable understanding of diversity will have to include (though in modern circumstances cannot be restricted to) religious commitments.

The problem should now be obvious: Any liberal argument that invokes autonomy as a general rule of public action in effect takes sides in the ongoing struggle between reason and faith, reflection and tradition. Autonomy-based arguments are bound to marginalize those individuals and groups who cannot conscientiously embrace the Enlightenment

19 The following discussion makes it crystal clear that in deploying the rubric of the "post-Reformation project," I am *not* (pace Brian Barry) invoking or endorsing the principle of one state-enforced religion for each political community. For Barry's remarks to the contrary, see *Culture and Equality* (Cambridge, Mass.: Harvard University Press, 2001), pp. 125–128.

impulse. To the extent that many liberals identify liberalism with the Enlightenment, they limit support for their cause and drive many citizens of goodwill – indeed, many potential allies – into opposition. It would not be difficult to explain the vicissitudes of late-twentieth-century American progressive politics along these lines.

But, it may be objected, this embrace of the Enlightenment is unavoidable; the liberal state simply must take sides in these quarrels. I disagree; in my judgment, it would not only be possible but also far preferable for liberals to take their bearings from the post-Reformation endeavor to make our common life safe for legitimate diversity. Liberal life, as I understand, makes place for the Enlightenment impulse as one important possibility but need not – indeed, must not – officially endorse Enlightenment values over all others.

To say that the liberal state should refrain from sponsoring Enlightenment values is not to say that it is or can be a neutral state, fully open to every form of life. There is no such polity, among other reasons, every political community is a sharing in some conception of justice and the human good, and this sharing will inevitably limit and shape the human possibilities it contains. Still, there are significant differences among regimes in their degrees of openness to difference and in the disincentives they present for leading our lives in particular ways. It is one thing to be a Jew in largely Christian American, another in Islamic Iran, yet another in Nazi Germany.

To be sure, the post-Reformation project, which of necessity distinguishes between politics and religion, may stack the decks in favor of certain kinds of religion (Protestant inwardness and, in general, faith-communities as opposed to law-communities). But even here it leaves room (as we will see) for substantial religious exercise, not just rights of conscience. Life in the United States may make it difficult for Orthodox Jews to perform all 613 of their commandments, let alone persuade their children to do so; but few if any acts explicitly commanded by Judaism are directly prohibited by the civil laws of the United States.

TAKING DIVERSITY SERIOUSLY

The post-Reformation project, which takes deep diversity as its point of departure, offers the best hope for maximizing opportunities for individuals and groups to lead lives as they see fit. But why should we want to take diversity so seriously? Let me suggest three kinds of arguments that might produce an overlapping consensus in favor of such a stance.

First, as Rawls has argued, we may feel compelled to acknowledge wide diversity as a *fact* that could be significantly altered only through the employment of unacceptable degrees of state coercion, with unacceptable levels of civil strife. Second, we may accept diversity as an *instrumental value*, on either Millian grounds that the existence of visible alternatives enhances the meaning of particular commitment or on Madisonian grounds that the multiplication of sects is the surest social obstacle to sectarian tyranny. Finally, we may embrace diversity as an *intrinsic value*. One variant of this is the thesis long urged by Isaiah Berlin, that our moral universe is characterized by plural and conflicting values that cannot be harmonized in a single comprehensive way of life; on this account, a wide (though not indefinitely wide) range of such goals and conceptions could serve as bases of worthwhile lives. Another form of the argument for intrinsic diversity appeals to the necessarily diverse experiences and standpoints of different groups within a complex social structure and to the desirability of public institutions that conduce to the expression, rather than the coercive suppression or covert homogenization, of such differences. It is to the theoretical basis for the intrinsic value of diversity that I now turn.

THREE SOURCES OF LIBERAL PLURALISM

THE RESOURCES OF LIBERAL THEORY

I spoke earlier of the resources liberal theory can bring to bear on the adjudication of disputes between state power and individual freedom. Three concepts are of particular importance: expressive liberty, value pluralism, and political pluralism.

Expressive Liberty

The first concept is what I call "expressive liberty." By this I mean the absence of constraints, imposed by some individuals on others, that make it impossible (or significantly more difficult) for the affected individuals to live their lives in ways that express their deepest beliefs about what gives meaning or value to life.[1] An example of such constraints would be the consequences of the Inquisition for Iberian Jews, who were forced either to endure persecution or renounce their religious practices.

Expressive liberty offers the opportunity to enjoy a fit between inner and outer, belief and practice. Not all sets of practices will themselves rest on, or reflect a preference for, liberty as ordinarily understood. For example, being Jewish is not always (indeed, is not usually) a matter of choice. But once that fact is established through birth and circumstance, it becomes a matter of great importance for Jews to live in a society

---

1 Expressive liberty constitutes the portion of negative liberty that bears directly on questions of identity. So understood, it implies a reasonable basis for distinguishing between those liberties that stand in a significant relation to living our identity and those that do not. Expressive liberty also requires some basis for arguing that the liberties it comprises are weighty relative to others. While the account I offer in the following paragraphs moves in this direction, there is much more to be said on these topics.

that permits them to live in accordance with their understanding of an identity that is given rather than chosen, and that typically is structured by commandments whose binding power does not depend on individual acceptance. Expressive liberty protects the ability of individuals and groups to live in ways that others would regard as unfree.

Expressive liberty is an important value because for most people, it is a precondition for leading lives they can experience as complete and satisfying. Part of what it means to have sincere beliefs about how one should live is the desire to live in accordance with them. It is only in rare cases (perhaps certain kinds of stoicism) that constraints imposed by other individuals and social structures do not affect the ability of believers to act on their convictions. For most of us, impediments to acting on our deepest beliefs are experienced as sources of deprivation and unhappiness, resentment and anger. Expressive liberty is a human good because its absence is an occasion for misfortunes that few would willingly endure.

Although expressive liberty is a good, it is not the only good, and it is certainly not unlimited. It does not protect every act flowing from sincere belief – human sacrifice, for example. But it does protect a range of practices that many will regard as objectionable – for example, the male circumcision and gender separation commanded by Orthodox Judaism.

Expressive liberty is possible only within societies whose members do not impede one another's opportunity to live their lives as they see fit. To be meaningful in practice, an ethics of liberty requires a sociology and a politics of liberty. Institutional arrangements can help police a zone of mutual abstention. But these institutions cannot succeed in the absence of pervasive belief that it is wrong to deprive others of their expressive liberties. Expressive liberty has civic preconditions – in particular, internalized norms of self-restraint when faced with practices that reflect understandings of the good life you do not share. Fostering this self-restraint, a core liberal virtue, is (within limits) a legitimate object of state action.

Value Pluralism

Expressive liberty would not be very significant if the zone of legitimate beliefs and practices were narrow – that is, if the moral considerations that lead us to forbid human sacrifice also rule out a wide range of other practices and limit us to a single conception of the human good. But this does not seem to be the case. I have come to believe that something along the lines of Isaiah Berlin's moral pluralism offers the best account of the moral universe we inhabit. He depicts a world in which fundamental values are plural, conflicting, incommensurable in theory, and uncombinable in practice – a world in which there is no single, univocal summum bonum that can be defined philosophically, let alone imposed politically.

A handful of propositions will clarify the basic thrust of value pluralism.

1. Value pluralism is offered as an account of the actual structure of the normative universe. It advances a truth-claim about that structure, not a description of the perplexity we feel in the face of divergent accounts of what is valuable. So value pluralism is not to be confused with emotivism, noncognitivism, or Humean arguments against the rational status of moral propositions. Like monism, it advances a "realist claim about the metaphysical structure of value."[2]

2. Pluralism is not the same as relativism. Philosophical reflection supports what ordinary experience suggests – a nonarbitrary distinction between good and bad or good and evil. For pluralism as for any serious position, the difference between (say) saving innocent lives and shedding innocent blood is part of the objective structure of the valuational universe. This provides a rational basis for defining a domain of basic moral decency for individual lives and for societies, roughly corresponding to H. L. A. Hart's conception of the minimum content of natural law.[3] As Stuart Hampshire puts it, "There are obvious limits set by common human needs to the conditions under which human beings flourish and human societies flourish. History records many ways of life which have crossed these limits."[4]

3. Above this domain of basic goods are found a multiplicity of genuine goods that are qualitatively heterogeneous and cannot be reduced to a common measure of value. Not all goods are moral (in any of the possible senses of that term). From an Aristotelian perspective, for example, goods other than the virtues or goods of the soul – goods of

---

2 Glen Newey, "Value-Pluralism in Contemporary Liberalism," *Dialogue* 37 (1998): 499.
3 H. L. A. Hart, *The Concept of Law* (Oxford: Clarendon, 1961), pp. 189–195.
4 Stuart Hampshire, *Morality and Conflict* (Cambridge, Mass.: Harvard University Press, 1983), p. 155.

the body, material resources, family and friends, a long and fortunate life – are also genuine goods. And heterogeneity exists not only between, but also within, the spheres of moral and nonmoral goods. The effort to designate a single measure of value either flattens out qualitative differences or (as in John Stuart Mill's version of utilitarianism) embraces these differences in all but name.

4. These qualitatively distinct values cannot be fully rank-ordered; there is no summum bonum that enjoys a rationally grounded priority for all individuals. This is not to say that it would be unreasonable for a particular individual to organize his or her life around a single dominant good, but only that there is no rational basis for extending that decision to, or imposing it on, others who understand their lives differently.

5. No single good or value, or set of goods or values, is overriding in all cases for the purpose of guiding action. Even if A is by some standard loftier or nobler than B, it may be the case that B is more urgent than A in specific circumstances, and it may be reasonable to give priority to urgency over nobility for decisions that must be made in those circumstances.

Contemporary value pluralists are committed both to affirming the heterogeneity of values and to denying the existence of comprehensive rank-orders among them. It is perfectly possible to assert heterogeneity without repudiating ranking. For example, while Aristotle argued (against Plato) that no single sense of goodness can be predicated of the many different kinds of things we regard as good, he was nonetheless prepared to rank goods on such grounds as completeness, self-sufficiency, and finality: Honor is subordinated to virtue because we seek to be honored for our virtue, and so forth (*Nicomachean Ethics* I. v–vi). To take a contemporary example, while Rawls does not reduce what we rightly care about to a single measure of value, he gives some values (those in the first principle of justice) lexical priority over others.

Value pluralists are prepared to acknowledge that the relationships among values may be structured in specific ways by the content of those values, but they reject the idea of a once-and-for-all priority of some values over others, regardless of circumstances and regardless of the sacrifices of value required by such strict priority rules. Nor can they accept the idea of a single summum bonum toward which all other goods are somehow directed. Certain partial orderings of goods are possible:

Many activities within military organizations are in the service of victory on the battlefield, the various arts of construction are subordinate to architecture, and so forth (*Nicomachean Ethics* I. 1). But value pluralists resist the conclusion that these partial orderings may themselves be combined into a single dominant ordering valid for all individuals and all circumstances. We may judge that Mozart was a better composer than Salieri, but on what scale of value could we compare Mozart's music to Rousseau's philosophy?

It is difficult to know what would constitute a definitive case in favor of value pluralism (or, for that matter, in favor of any other general view of our moral lives). But it is possible to survey the most important considerations that make value pluralism plausible and to blunt the force of some key objections to it.

Many philosophers argue for value pluralism by pointing to the multiplicity of sources of morality (or types of moral reasons). For example, Charles Larmore suggests that there are three kinds of valid moral claims – particularistic duties, aggregate consequences, and universal ("deontological") rules of conduct – that cannot be reduced to a common measure and whose relative weight depends on circumstances.[5] To this list Thomas Nagel adds two others: "perfectionist" claims based on the intrinsic value of certain achievements and creations, and claims based on commitments to personal projects and undertakings, especially core commitments that help define our identities.[6]

Unresolvable conflicts may break out, not only between but also within types of claims. Some general duties may clash with others (so may ideals), and we may find ourselves torn between powerful particularist obligations, as when we must somehow choose between our children and our parents.[7]

To be sure, these descriptive claims in favor of value pluralism are not definitive. Many choices confront us with practically incompatible alternatives, each of which is valuable. The fact that when we choose

5 Charles Larmore, *Patterns of Moral Complexity* (Cambridge: Cambridge University Press, 1987), Chapter 6.
6 Thomas Nagel, "The Fragmentation of Value," in *Mortal Questions* (Cambridge: Cambridge University Press, 1979), pp. 129–130.
7 Charles Larmore, *The Morals of Modernity* (Cambridge: Cambridge University Press, 1996), pp. 157–163; Steven Lukes, "Making Sense of Moral Conflict," in *Moral Conflict and Politics* (Oxford: Clarendon Press, 1991).

we must exclude something of genuine value is a source of regret. But we cannot infer value pluralism from the bare fact of regret, because the course of action we choose may embody the same value as the course we reject. And even when the alternatives seem to involve heterogeneous values, it is logically possible that a convinced monist could redescribe them in light of an encompassing common value.[8]

These philosophical possibilities are less compelling, however, than are the phenomena of heterogeneity they seek to explain away. This becomes clear when we move from the abstract concept of monism to a concrete conception – namely, the species of utilitarianism that understands what is to be maximized as want-satisfaction.[9] As Brian Barry observes, the difficulty is that it requires some people to "accept a way of regarding their own conceptions of the good that they could reasonably find repugnant." Someone who opposes the construction of a dam on the grounds that the species of animal thereby destroyed has intrinsic value would rightly resist the claim that his belief is nothing more than a want to be satisfied: "[T]o say that he can keep his conception of the good, but only on condition that the conclusions he reaches on the basis of it are to be treated as wants and aggregated with other people's wants, is really saying that he cannot keep it."[10] From a Rawlsian perspective, utilitarianism fails to take seriously the separateness of persons. From a pluralist perspective, however, the core problem is that utilitarianism fails to take seriously the heterogeneity of values. The burden of proof is on utilitarians (and ethical monists of all kinds) to show how the apparent diversity of values can be translated into a single vocabulary of value without loss of moral meaning.

Although pluralist philosophers point to the implausibility of reductionist arguments on the plane of theory, it is concrete experience that provides the most compelling reasons for accepting some form of value pluralism. Not infrequently, our lives present conflicts of goods or values that seem fundamental but heterogeneous, with no evident basis for comparison and choice. Recall Sartre's example of the young man torn

---

8 Newey, "Value-Pluralism in Contemporary Liberalism," pp. 500–504.

9 This is, of course, only one variant of utilitarianism, selected to illustrate the thesis. The argument in the text would have to be altered to address other forms of utilitarianism, although the broad thrust of the critique remains intact.

10 Brian Barry, *A Treatise on Social Justice*, Volume 2: *Justice as Impartiality* (Oxford: Clarendon Press, 1995), pp. 162–163.

between his mother and the French resistance. Or consider the choice faced by members of the resistance itself: attacking German soldiers and officials with the near certainty of prompting retaliation against uninvolved French civilians, or accepting the oppressive terms of the occupation. In history's rearview mirror, we see the heroism of the resistance magnified. But in the eyes of many ordinary people at the time, the balance of values was by no means obvious.

In this respect, public life mirrors the structure of private life. During policy disputes, the contending forces typically appeal to competing goods and principles, each of which has prima facie moral weight. In many cases, there is no obvious way of reducing these diverse considerations to a common measure of value or of giving one kind of claim lexical priority over others. The most difficult political choices are not between good and bad but between good and good.

In these cases, as with more abstract philosophical arguments, one may question the inference from the appearance of heterogeneity to the moral or metaphysical fact. Might it not be possible to redescribe the clash of apparently diverse values as a conflict between mutually exclusive efforts to achieve the same value? Perhaps so; but these cases differ fundamentally from the choice between (say) going to the theater and going out to dinner with a friend, mutually exclusive ways of realizing the good of a pleasurable evening.[11] It is not at all clear what the value that overarches loyalty to one's mother and fighting for the freedom of one's country might be. Here again, the burden of proof falls on would-be monists to move beyond the abstract possibility of common values. They must specify such values and show how these values do justice to the moral experiences they seek to redescribe.

It is important not to overdramatize the choices flowing from the heterogeneity of value. To be sure, there are extreme ("tragic") circumstances in which we may feel that we are forced altogether to set aside morally significant considerations. These are the situations in which we are apt to feel guilty, sullied, or regretful even if we believe we have done the right thing, all things considered. But typically, values admit of more and less; the practical issue is the weight to be attached to competing values, the balance to be struck among them. Nor is it the

11 Newey, "Value-Pluralism in Contemporary Liberalism," p. 500.

case that choices involving heterogeneous values are always rationally underdetermined. Value pluralism does not rule out the possibility of compelling (if nonalgorithmic) arguments for right answers in specific situations.[12] So value pluralists are not committed to the view that disputes over value are "rationally interminable," and the unresolvability of such disputes is not in itself evidence in favor of value pluralism. The point is rather the observed structure of the many value conflicts that do not appeal to a shared good or value and cannot be resolved by quantitative claims of the form that option A is more promotive of the (shared) good or value than is option B.

The underlying philosophical point, first suggested by Brian Barry three decades ago, is that fundamental values can be comparable even if not commensurable. Deliberative argument can provide reasons for choices among qualitatively different claims even when no common measure of value is available.[13] As Michael Stocker observes, the worry that plural values make rational judgment and action impossible – in the absence of algorithmic ways of comparing these values – comes not from reflection on how we actually judge and act, but from top-down philosophic assumptions about how the process of judgment must work. The fact that we judge and choose without such measures or rules shows either that these assumptions are misguided "or that our judgements and choices are almost all arbitrary and unreasoned."[14] But there is no good reason to endorse this pessimistic conclusion about reasonable judgment, and therefore a strong reason to embrace an account of nonalgorithmic but reasonable choice based on qualitative considerations. That is all that pluralist deliberation requires.

12 For an important discussion of these points within legal deliberation, see Cass Sunstein, "Incommensurability and Valuation in Law," *Michigan Law Review* 92, 4 (1994): 779–861.

13 Brian Barry, *Political Argument: A Reissue with a New Introduction* (Berkeley: University of California Press, 1990), pp. 3–8. Barry's new introduction contains useful additional discussions of value comparability in relation to Rawls's account of intuitionism and lexical orderings; see especially pp. xxxix–xliv, lxix–lxxii. See also Larmore, *The Morals of Modernity*, pp. 157–163. The most rigorous account of incommensurability is probably Joseph Raz, *The Morality of Freedom* (Oxford: Clarendon Press, 1986), Chapter 13. But Raz drives this concept in a more existentialist direction than Barry or Larmore, arguing that incommensurability typically yields situations in which reason is incapable of guiding action (*The Morality of Freedom*, pp. 333–334).

14 Michael Stocker, *Plural and Conflicting Values* (Oxford: Clarendon Press, 1990), p. 194.

Political Pluralism

The political pluralism developed by early-twentieth-century British theorists, such as J. N. Figgis, G. D. H. Cole, and Harold Laski, provides a third source of support for the account of liberalism I am developing. For our purposes, the key idea offered by these thinkers was a critique of the plenipotentiary state, whether understood in an Aristotelian or Austinian manner. Instead, they argued our social life comprises multiple sources of authority and sovereignty – individuals, parents, associations, churches, and state institutions, among others – no one of which is dominant for all purposes and on all occasions. Nonstate authority does not exist simply as a concession or gift of the state. A well-ordered state recognizes, but does not create, other sources of authority.[15]

The theory of multiple sovereignties does not imply the existence of separate social spheres, each governed by its own form of authority. Political pluralism is consistent with the fact of overlapping authorities whose relationship to one another must somehow be worked out. For example, neither parents nor state institutions have unfettered power over the education of children. From a pluralist point of view, the state cannot rightly resolve educational disputes with parents by asserting the comprehensive authority of its conceptions over theirs. Nor can parents assert a comprehensive authority over the state when conflicts erupt over their children's education. Rather, the substance of particular controversies shapes our judgment concerning the appropriate allocation of decisional authority.

It is said that during medieval times, Bulan, king of the Khazers, summoned four wise men to his kingdom – a secular philosopher, a Christian scholar, a Moslem scholar, and a rabbi. After interrogating them seriatim on the content and basis of their beliefs, Bulan called his people together in an assembly, declared that he accepted Judaism, and decreed that all Khazers would thenceforth be instructed in and practice Judaism as their communal faith.[16]

---

15 For elaboration, see Paul Q. Hirst, ed., *The Pluralist Theory of the State: Selected Writings of G. D. H. Cole, J. N. Figgis, and H. J. Laski* (London: Routledge, 1989). Hirst's introduction offers an unusually clear guide to the central themes of pluralist thought.

16 See Jehuda Halevy, *Kuzari: The Book of Proof and Argument,* edited with an introduction and commentary by Isaak Heinemann (Oxford: East and West Library, 1947), pp. 50–51.

I suspect that this chain of events strikes most readers today as strange. Would it be less strange if – rather than one man deciding for all – the people had assembled themselves and, after the most scrupulous democratic deliberation, settled on Judaism as the official religion of the Khazer nation? I think not. There is a threshold question: Does the state possess the legitimate power to make collectively binding decisions on this matter? If not, the question of how such decisions should be made is never reached. From a pluralist perspective, religion is a clear example of a matter that is not subject to plenipotentiary state power.

In matters of this sort, individuals and civil associations are not required to give an account of – or justify – themselves before any public bar. So, for example, representatives of minority religions could not rightly be compelled by a congressional committee to explain the essentials of their faith. Indeed, as Ira Katznelson has recently argued, such individuals are not morally obligated to give an account of themselves to anyone, public or private: A meaningful pluralism entails "the right not to offer a reason for being different." Katznelson builds on Susan Mendus's metaphor of "neighborliness." We owe our neighbors civil behavior that is mindful of the impact on them of what we do, but ordinarily "neighbors do not owe each other reasons" for the way they choose to lead their lives.[17]

HOW THE SOURCES OF LIBERAL THEORY
FIT TOGETHER

I began by suggesting that there are three important but sometimes neglected resources on which liberal theory can draw. It remains to sketch the relationship among them.

I need not dwell on the relationship between expressive liberty and moral pluralism. Suffice it to say that if moral pluralism is the most nearly adequate depiction of the moral universe we inhabit, then the range of choiceworthy human lives is very wide. While some ways of life can be ruled out as violating minimum standards of humanity, most cannot. If so, then the zone of human agency protected by the norm of expressive liberty is capacious indeed. Moral pluralism supports the

17 Ira Katznelson, *Liberalism's Crooked Circle: Letters to Adam Michnik* (Princeton, N.J.: Princeton University Press, 1996), pp. 171–173. Katznelson takes the first quotation from an article by Patha Chatterjee.

importance of expressive liberty in ways that monistic theories of value or accounts of the summum bonum do not.

There is a relationship of mutual support between moral pluralism and political pluralism. Moral pluralism suggests that not all intrinsic goods are political goods; many are social, or private. These goods are heterogeneous. In particular, the goods of family, of social life, and of religion cannot be adequately understood as functionally related to the political order. These goods affect politics, but they do not exist only for the sake of politics. Not every religion cannot be reduced to "civil" religion; not every parental decision serves (or needs to serve) the common good. Because this heterogeneity of value precludes instrumental rank-ordering, political goods do not enjoy a comprehensive priority over others in every circumstance.

Moral pluralism lends support to the proposition that the state should not be regarded as all-powerful, while political pluralism helps define and defend the social space within which the heterogeneity of value can be translated into a rich variety of worthy human lives. This mutual support does not rule out all hierarchical relations between the state and other activities, however. In a free society with a multiplicity of individual and associational beliefs, practices that give expression to these beliefs are bound to come into conflict. In some cases, the contending parties will be able to negotiate some accommodation.

But not always. State power can legitimately regulate the terms of the relationship among social agents, provided that the public structure is as fair as possible to all and allows ample opportunities for expressive liberty. In this respect, unlike others, the state enjoys a certain priority: It is the key source of order in a system of ordered liberty.

4

LIBERAL PLURALIST THEORY

Comprehensive, Not Political

THE REJECTION OF COMPREHENSIVE THEORY
AS A BASIS FOR POLITICAL THEORY

Even if value pluralism is accepted as the most adequate comprehensive account of the structure of the valuational universe, one may deny that this theory of value has any relevance to political philosophy. John Rawls has argued that arguments in support of fundamental political values must be decoupled from comprehensive doctrines. This is because "a basic feature of democracy is the fact of reasonable pluralism – the fact that a plurality of conflicting reasonable comprehensive doctrines, religious, philosophical, and moral, is the normal result of its culture of free institutions. Citizens realize that they cannot reach agreement or even approach mutual understanding on the basis of their irreconcilable comprehensive doctrines."[1]

This fact, Rawls argues, is fraught with moral significance. When citizens offer one another reasons for mutually binding forms of social organization and cooperation, they should confine themselves to "political values that others, as free and equal citizens might also reasonably be expected reasonably to endorse."[2] If they do not, the proposed decisions tacitly deny the freedom and equality of citizens who feel conscientiously impelled to oppose those decisions.[3] Reasons appealing to comprehensive conceptions rejected by one's fellow citizens violate this requirement, and public justifications of basic public institutions and policies must therefore avoid them. Instead, public reasons should

---

1 John Rawls, "The Idea of Public Reason Revisited," *University of Chicago Law Review* 64, 3 (1997): 765–766.
2 Ibid., p. 773.
3 Ibid., p. 770.

appeal to freestanding political values, such as those mentioned in the Preamble to the Constitution – the common defense, general welfare, domestic tranquility, and so forth.[4]

Rawls does distinguish, however, between the political sphere and what he terms the background culture (roughly coextensive with what others call civil society). In the former, citizens are obliged to confine their proposed justifications to public reason. In the latter, we are free to employ our preferred comprehensive doctrines as the basis of argument.[5] The basis of this distinction seems to be that unlike the political sphere, civil society does not exercise coercive power over fellow citizens. It follows that it is legitimate for scholars acting in their "civil," rather than directly "political," capacity to investigate the relationship between the comprehensive doctrines they take to be true and specific political ideals or institutions.

WHY WE SHOULD QUESTION THE REJECTION OF COMPREHENSIVE THEORY

Rawls's account raises two issues. First, is it possible for political speech among citizens to remain within public reason, as Rawls defines it? And second, what are the implications of his account for the practice of political philosophy?

Public Reason among Citizens

It is doubtful that the constitutional values Rawls presents as freestanding public reasons can be adequately understood as detached from comprehensive views. After all, the Preamble begins and ends by asserting the right of the people (and, by implication, *only* the people) to ordain and establish the Constitution. This was a revolutionary assertion of the basic republican principle, not at that time generally accepted in the West. This principle drew its support from the kinds of premises Jefferson summarized in the Declaration of Independence – premises that, taken together, sketch what Rawls would have to call a comprehensive view. Human beings are equal because they are created equal; they are free because they are endowed with certain rights that cannot

4 Ibid., p. 776.
5 Ibid., p. 768.

be taken away; and because they are free and equal, governments can only derive their just powers from the consent of the governed.

It is true that after political institutions have functioned for some time, their legitimacy may come to be taken for granted, and their constitutive values may come to be seen as freestanding. But this is an illusion, quickly dispelled in times of internal or external crisis. Slavery drove President Lincoln to philosophical arguments for human equality, and the Civil War drove him to theological reflections on divine judgment. The antidemocratic threats of the twentieth century moved Western democracies toward moral universalism, expressed in the Nuremberg trials and the Universal Declaration of Human Rights.

It is not only systemic challenges that evoke comprehensive public discourse; constitutional and policy disputes may do so as well. Even if we take our bearings from public constitutional values, the interpretation of general concepts, such as the "general welfare" and the "blessings of liberty," is bound to reflect competing, contestable moral understandings. Some will argue that the general welfare means the greatest good of the greatest number; others will insist, against Berlin, that liberty includes positive as well as negative elements; and so forth. Differences of moral doctrine will come into play when rights conflict, or when rights-based claims collide with the requirements of consequentialism.

On the level of policy, consider the widespread practice of depriving certain convicted felons of the right to vote, even after their release from incarceration. They have been deprived of a fundamental attribute of citizenship; they are less than equal citizens, in some cases permanently so. If this policy is legitimate, it reveals (and rests on) certain assumptions about the conduct expected of persons if they are to remain within the sphere of equal citizenship.

Or consider what Rawls terms "an easy case" – religious liberty: Not only must Servetus understand why Calvin wanted to burn him at the stake; Calvin's reasons must be reasonably acceptable to Servetus.[6] The difficulty is that even defensible restraints on religious practices can fail to meet this stricture. Suppose a religious group claims the right to practice human sacrifice, with the informed and carefully verified consent of all involved. The potential sacrificial offerings may believe that their role in core ritual observances of their faith will qualify them for spiritual

6 Ibid., p. 771.

goods (salvation, or a life of everlasting bliss) they regard as being of incomparable worth. Citizens who wish to forbid this practice are forced either to deny the truth of this claim or to affirm the priority of certain public goods (for example, preserving life) over the religious values the group seeks to pursue. In either case, those arguing for restraints on human sacrifice (just about all of us, one suspects) are compelled to take a position on the truth or weight of a comprehensive conception. To complicate matters further, many of those arguing for such restraints would not only oppose current laws against suicide but also favor legislation permitting physician-assisted suicide. They would have to set forth the principled reasons for allowing fellow citizens to consent to have their lives taken for physical but not spiritual reasons – not an easy task in the absence of considerations that are, in Rawls's sense, comprehensive rather than public.

As a general matter, it is not clear that Rawls's criterion of reasonable rejectability should govern public political justification. Many public policy decisions turn on contestable assessments of empirical evidence and of the results of scientific inquiry, yet it is not typically argued that coercive legislation is illegitimate whenever it overrides the reasonable empirical objections of some citizens. Other decisions will turn on competing interpretations of core public values, disagreements that bring into play the kinds of comprehensive claims that philosophers use to justify regime-types, such as liberal democracy. For example, Rawls's longstanding rejection of desert as a component of distributive justice rests on deep but eminently contestable propositions about the influence of social forces in shaping traits of character, such as the willingness to work hard and contribute what one can to the commonwealth.

The Conduct of Political Philosophy

Rawls's conception of public reason raises larger questions about the purposes of political philosophy. For most of its history, political philosophy engaged in the normative evaluation of regime-types. Comparisons among forms of kingship, aristocracy, republicanism, theocracy, and (more recently) ideologically based vanguard parties invoked or spilled over into "comprehensive" issues of ethics, human nature, philosophical psychology, epistemology, metaphysics, and religion. Conclusions about better and worse regimes – for particular situations and more generally – reflected these issues as well as more practical and political considerations.

This classic practice of political philosophy has not entirely disappeared. In *Democracy and Its Critics*, for example, Robert Dahl feels impelled both to refute the antidemocratic arguments of anarchism and guardianship and to offer affirmative arguments for the basic presuppositions of democracy. In Dahl's view, democratic theory "depends on assumptions and premises that uncritical advocates have shied away from exploring, or in some cases even openly acknowledging." His aim is to drag this "shadow theory" into the sunlight and explore the extent to which it can be rationally defended,[7] a goal that leads him to explore theories of moral autonomy and basic human interests, among others.[8]

Rawls proceeds entirely differently. He takes democracy – more precisely, liberal constitutional democracy – as his point of departure. This enables him to set aside the arguments that undergird democracy and to treat its basic elements as freestanding "political" conceptions. He may be seen as engaged in a hypothetical-conceptual mode of argument: If we accept democracy, then A, B, C, ... N are aspects of our commitment, and Rawls's conception of public reason is one such aspect. So understood, this argument will be compelling only to those who are disposed (for whatever reason) to conduct politics within a democratic frame. It is not an argument for democracy; public reason and democracy stand or fall together. As Rawls says, the idea of public reason "does not engage" those who reject constitutional democracy.[9]

The hypothetical-conceptual claim is far from trivial. The assertion that liberal constitutional democracy implies or requires the practice of Rawlsian public reason is important if true. And it is not without intuitive plausibility. Many citizens (not just militant secularists) resist what they see as sectarian public arguments – those resting on a "literal" interpretation of the Bible, for example. Still, many other citizens see arguments confined to secular-constitutional values as themselves sectarian. And as we have seen, there are reasons to doubt whether political discourse confined to freestanding public reasons is even possible.

---

7 Robert Dahl, *Democracy and Its Critics* (New Haven, Conn.: Yale University Press, 1989), pp. 2–3.
8 Ibid., Chapters 6 and 7.
9 Rawls, "The Idea of Public Reason Revisited," pp. 766–767.

It is not clear, however, that Rawls's argument is limited to hypothetical-conceptual claims. Comprehensive doctrines are deemed "unreasonable" to the extent that they stand in tension with constitutional democracy,[10] inviting us to believe that the rejection of democracy is itself unreasonable. If this is what Rawls means, then he must offer reasons to show why there is no basis for accepting nondemocratic modes of governance. Because the idea of public reason is parasitic on democracy, it cannot be used against those who question democracy. Those who invoke comprehensive doctrines against democratic governance and liberties must be met on their own ground; the evidence provided by those doctrines cannot be ruled out as inadmissible. The alternative is stubborn silence, a kind of democratic dogmatism that ill serves both theory and practice.

On Rawls's own account, there is no reason that scholars acting in a civil capacity cannot provide comprehensive defenses of democracy as, for example, Dahl does. But Rawls conspicuously refrains from exercising his civil rights as a political philosopher. He treats democracy as a fixed point, as a premise from which conclusions flow but for which no arguments are advanced. In so doing, he invites, perhaps inadvertently, the misunderstanding to which many of those who accept his approach have succumbed – that even within political philosophy, it is inappropriate to offer comprehensive arguments in favor of regimes such as liberal constitutional democracy.

Consider the argument advanced by Charles Larmore against using Berlinian value pluralism as a basis for liberalism: The aim of political liberalism is to find principles that reasonable people can accept, regardless of their particular comprehensive conceptions of the good. Value pluralism is far too controversial to be counted among these principles; individuals may be regarded as reasonable even though they reject the pluralist account of the good.[11] And it is unreasonable to ask individuals to subscribe to binding principles of political association (not to mention coercive legislation) on the basis of claims that they can reasonably reject.

Whatever the merits of this argument, it does not make a compelling case against using value pluralism as part of a philosophical justification

---

10 Ibid., pp. 766.
11 Charles Larmore, *The Morals of Modernity* (Cambridge: Cambridge University Press, 1996), pp. 154–155, 173–174.

for liberalism. To be sure, the considerations adduced in favor of value pluralism are not definitive. But there are domains of inquiry in which it is unreasonable to reject less than conclusive propositions. The exclusion of valid but reasonably rejectable claims would eviscerate practical philosophy.

Rawls's reasonable rejectability criterion gains intuitive force from the relation between religion and politics. For various reasons, it has come to appear implausible that general public principles (or specific policies) should rest on propositions derived from a particular revealed tradition – even if we assume for the sake of argument that these propositions are true.

So Rawls's understanding accords with widely held beliefs, up to a point. His originality lies in extending restraints on the public use of theology to include secular moral doctrines, which are, he says, "on a level with religion and first philosophy."[12]

This assertion raises a number of issues. In the first place, it is far from clear that it makes sense to assimilate moral doctrines into religion. While the gap between faith and reason is not as wide as many assume, revelation presumes an experience potentially available to all, but not actually received by all. By contrast, secular moral doctrines rest their claims on shared experience and uncontroversial canons of reasoning. Debates among (say) utilitarians, Kantians, perfectionists, particularists, and pluralists are conducted on common ground and are potentially resolvable in a way that disagreements between Christians and Jews are not. For the civil conduct of political philosophy, it would seem appropriate to debate – and when warranted employ – premises drawn from secular moral arguments.

Nor is it clear that political philosophy can exclude comprehensive philosophy without succumbing to dogmatism or historical determinism. Throughout the twentieth century and down to the present, various regimes have denied the basic premises of liberal constitutional democracy. Some may assume that we have reached an unprecedented moment at which it is no longer necessary to take such challenges seriously. It would be more modest, and safer, to assume that a traditional task of political philosophy – defining and defending the difference between better and worse forms of political organization – remains relevant today.

12 Rawls, "The Idea of Public Reason Revisited," pp. 775–776.

If so, democratic philosophers had better be prepared to articulate the premises on which the superiority of democratic practices is held to rest. They cannot hope to do this simply by gesturing toward the stock of assumptions taken for granted within democratic societies.

Rawls wants political philosophy to proceed by elaborating widely held values, such as the freedom and equality of citizens and society as a system of social cooperation. But moving from broad concepts to more determinate conceptions is bound to bring controversial moral theories into play. For example, Rawls has long argued that taking moral desert into account for purposes of distribution denies the premises of democratic citizenship. Others have replied that it is Rawls's argument for excluding desert that violates those premises, by denying the capacity of individuals to act freely and, thus, to be held responsible for the consequences of their acts. Brian Barry notes that the response since 1971 to Rawls's argument has been "overwhelmingly negative"[13] – rightly so, in my judgment. But even if one agrees with Rawls, the point is that philosophers cannot even enter this argument (on either side) without deploying claims that Rawls seeks to exclude from public reason.

REASONABLE DISAGREEMENT AND VALUE PLURALISM

Larmore wants to argue both that it is wrong for public reason to rely on contestable moral theories such as value pluralism and right to respect the criterion of reasonable disagreement. The problem is that the two cannot be cleanly separated. Rawls traces the inevitability of reasonable disagreement to what he calls the "burdens of reason." But of the half dozen specific "burdens" he cites, three overlap with key theses of value pluralism: Different kinds of normative considerations may be involved on both sides of a question; when we are forced to select among cherished values, we find it hard to set priorities; even when the choice involves balancing rather than choosing among important values, we may well disagree about their weight.[14] To be sure, other factors are at work: empirical conflicts and complexities; vague concepts with uncertain boundaries and applications; and the diversity of formative individual experiences in highly differentiated modern societies. Still, on

---

13 Brian Barry, *Political Argument: A Reissue with a New Introduction* (Berkeley: University of California Press, 1990), p. lvii.

14 Larmore, *The Morals of Modernity*, p. 170.

Rawls's own view, it is not clear that we could take moral disagreement to be inevitable among reasonable persons in circumstances of liberty unless we accept some version of value pluralism.

Larmore denies this because he takes disagreement to be the expected result (if you will, the default position) of unfettered human thought in every sphere, not just morals or metaphysics or religion. On this account, we do not make progress in the natural sciences because we have managed to get on the track of truth. Rather, convergence on scientific truth is simply "what a community of investigators will accept when they agree to subject their observation of nature to forms of reasoning designed to secure agreement."[15] But this fashionable constructivist view of the scientific process is hard to accept. What keeps socially constructed scientific agreement in reasonable proximity to nature, so that theory-based predictions about natural events can be observationally supported or falsified? It seems more sensible to suggest that the deep structure of the natural world differs fundamentally from the corresponding structure of the moral world. To repeat, this is not to offer a relativist or subjectivist account of valuation; value pluralism claims to describe (not construct) the basic structure of the moral world we actually inhabit – a description that both explains and (within limits) justifies the pervasiveness of moral disagreement. The point is that we cannot explain the difference between disagreement in science and in morality – and, therefore, the requirement of accepting a substantial range of diversity in politics – without adverting to the kinds of philosophical claims that Rawls, Larmore, and others seek to exclude from the domains both of political philosophy and of public argument among citizens.

15 Ibid., p. 171.

5

FROM VALUE PLURALISM TO LIBERAL PLURALIST POLITICS

I have argued that there are good reasons to accept value pluralism as the best account of the moral universe we inhabit, and no good reason to reject comprehensive theory as a part of our motivation for embracing a political theory. This leaves open the question of what the implications of value pluralism for political theory may be. I begin my answer to this question by exploring the disagreement between John Gray and the late Isaiah Berlin.

THE POLITICAL IMPLICATIONS OF VALUE PLURALISM: JOHN GRAY VERSUS ISAIAH BERLIN

Isaiah Berlin is famous for an account of liberalism resting on two master-ideas: value pluralism and negative liberty, understood as the capacity of individuals, unimpeded by external coercion or constraint, to choose for themselves among competing conceptions of good or valuable lives.[1] In a series of recent writings, John Gray argues that these two master-ideas do not fit together. The more seriously we take value pluralism, the less inclined we will be to give pride of place to negative liberty as a good that trumps all others. We will certainly not be able to accord negative liberty anything like lexical priority. We will accept that lives defined by habit, tradition, or the acceptance of authority can be valid forms of human flourishing, and that forms of political association organized to defend groups practicing these ways of life are themselves legitimate. We will therefore recognize that liberalism – understood as

---

1 Isaiah Berlin, *Four Essays on Liberty* (Oxford: Oxford University Press, 1969), Chapter 3.

the philosophy of societies in which negative liberty takes pride of place – enjoys only local authority. If Berlin's account of value pluralism is correct, Gray concludes, liberal democracy cannot sustain its universalist claims and emerges as but one form (among many others) of valid political association.[2]

Gray is right to resist efforts to rest liberalism on the value of autonomy. As I argued in Chapter 2, from a value-pluralist standpoint, there are many valuable ways of life, individual and collective, that are not autonomous in the sense that they are not the product of conscious reflection and choice but, rather, of habit, tradition, authority, or unswerving faith. The question is whether the pluralist critique of autonomy (and more generally, of theories of positive liberty) extends to negative liberty.

One thing is clear at the outset: Berlin himself did not think so. Daniel Weinstock offers a useful distinction between "radical" and "restricted" pluralism. In the radical version, any objective value can in principle be replaced by any other, and any combination of objective values is acceptable. In the restricted version of pluralism, by contrast, some values are not wholly replaceable. For Berlin, negative liberty was one such value:

We must preserve a minimum area of personal freedom if we are not to "degrade or deny our nature." We cannot remain absolutely free, and must give up some of our liberty to preserve the rest. But total self-surrender is self-defeating. What then must the minimum be? That which a man cannot give up without offending against the essence of human nature.[3]

Berlin is drawn to the Romantic/historicist view of human beings as individually and collectively self-creating. Contrary to the teachings of classic philosophical and theological traditions, human nature does not prescribe a single, generally valid model of human flourishing or perfection. But to say that human nature underdetermines how we can live as human beings is not to say that it has no bearing on this question. As Weinstock puts it, "self-creation occurs within certain conceptual limits."[4]

2 John Gray, *Isaiah Berlin* (Princeton, N.J.: Princeton University Press, 1996), Chapter 6.
3 Berlin, *Four Essays on Liberty*, p. 126; see also Steven Lukes, "The Singular and the Plural: On the Distinctive Liberalism of Isaiah Berlin," *Social Research* 61, 3: 711–714.
4 Daniel Weinstock, "The Graying of Berlin," *Critical Review* 11, 4 (1997): 490.

To be sure, Berlin is less clear than he might be as to the source and status of these limits. Phrases such as the "essence of human nature" gesture toward philosophical psychology or metaphysical accounts of natural law. To these grounding possibilities Berlin immediately and explicitly adds utilitarianism, natural rights theories, the categorical imperative, and the social contract tradition.[5] Elsewhere, Berlin offers an apparently historical account of "rules so long and widely accepted that their observance has entered into the very conception of what it is to be a normal human being."[6] Unlike metaphysics, the historical account would seem to leave open the possibility that long-cycle changes in human experience could slowly revise even entrenched views about the existence of frontiers delimiting zones of human inviolability.[7] But we need not resolve these ambiguities to conclude that a measure of negative liberty enters into Berlin's understanding of the moral threshold below which no form of life can be considered minimally human, decent, and morally acceptable.

Gray is in no position to reject the possibility of such a role for negative liberty. He recognizes in Berlin's thought the presence of a minimal universalism that can be deployed against the political excesses of the twentieth century – in particular, against those doctrines that sought to liberate political action from the constraints of even the minimum content of morality. And he acknowledges the moral force of this common moral horizon of the species: Regimes are illegitimate, he says, unless their members achieve the "minimal conditions of decency among themselves."[8] The challenge is to specify the content of these conditions. As we shall see, Gray's arguments against including a measure of negative liberty among these conditions are less than compelling.

The core of Berlinian negative liberty is the absence of external coercion. The essence of unfreedom is imprisonment; Berlin declares that "the fundamental sense of freedom is freedom from chains, from imprisonment, from enslavement, by others. The rest is an extension of this sense, or else metaphor."[9]

5 Berlin, *Four Essays on Liberty*, p. 127.
6 Ibid., p. 165.
7 For a discerning discussion of these and related matters, see Claude J. Galipeau, *Isaiah Berlin's Liberalism* (Oxford: Clarendon Press, 1994), pp. 48–71.
8 Gray, *Isaiah Berlin*, pp. 157–158, 168.
9 Berlin, *Four Essays on Liberty*, p. lvi.

From the standpoint of negative liberty, the crucial issue is not the belief system or psychology that leads individuals to particular ways of life but, rather, the absence of force (or threats backed by force). The surest sign of unfreedom occurs when individuals are coerced to remain in ways of life they wish to leave. The politics of negative liberty seeks, first and foremost, to protect their ability to leave – although not necessarily to cultivate the awareness and reflective powers that may stimulate the desire to leave.

Notably, Berlin does not straightforwardly equate what I have called the politics of negative liberty with the institutions of modern democracy. Negative liberty, he declares, "is not incompatible with some kinds of autocracy, or at any rate with the absence of self-government." Conversely, "a democracy may, in fact, deprive the individual citizen of a great many liberties which he might have in some other form of society." Berlin leaves open the possibility that self-government may in practice protect individual liberty better than other regimes. But the connection is empirical rather than logical: The concept of negative liberty occupies the endpoint of one continuum, and self-government the endpoint of a different continuum.[10]

So there is to be found in Berlin's thought some support for the wedge Gray wishes to drive between value pluralism and Western democracy. But Berlin's argument cannot be taken as far as Gray wishes to go, for two reasons. First, practical experience may well confirm what philosophy by itself cannot establish, that democratic institutions far more reliably protect negative liberties than do other forms of political organization. As recent events in China make clear, even nondemocratic polities with substantial market economies feel threatened by, and therefore tend to invade, bedrock negative liberties, such as freedom of religious conscience. Second, as we have seen, Berlin refuses to radicalize value pluralism so as to put negative liberty on all fours with other human goods. To be sure (as Berlin explicitly acknowledges), it is frequently necessary to balance negative liberty against other principles of social action, and even to allow these alternative principles to dominate negative liberty in decisions concerning specific institutions and policies.[11] But in the end, the fact of value pluralism itself gives special status to individual liberty. As Berlin puts it:

10 Ibid., pp. 129–130.
11 Ibid., p. 169.

The world that we encounter in ordinary experience is one in which we are with choices between ends equally ultimate, and claims equally absolute, the realization of some of which must inevitably involve the sacrifice of others. *Indeed, it is because this is their situation that men place such immense value upon the freedom to choose.*[12]

It is at this point that Gray enters a forceful dissent. There is, he says, no direct road from value pluralism to negative liberty. The reason is this: While every form of life represents a choice among possibilities, often

the forms of life so chosen are ones in which choice-making is accorded no special significance. The elevation of choice-making to a central place in the human good cannot, then, be a deduction from a universal feature of human life, namely the role that choosing has in making us the people we are; nor can it be derived from the pluralist thesis of value-incommensurability.[13]

What are we to make of this disagreement?

Let me begin by examining an attractive but incomplete argument advanced by Daniel Weinstock against Gray and in support of a link between pluralism and liberalism. The argument runs as follows:

On Gray's account of Berlin (which Gray himself endorses), value pluralism expresses a deep truth about the structure of the moral universe. Now consider two ideal-typical figures, Liberal and Traditional. Liberal lives her life in full awareness of the truth of value pluralism. She knows that her way of life, though a source of meaning and satisfaction, is but one among many defensible lives she might have led under other circumstances. She understands that her life represents what might be termed a selection of value; even if she inherited that life from her parents or community without systematic reflection on alternatives to it, she understands that her continued identification with it is in some real sense a choice. By contrast, to the extent that he is even aware of ways of life other than his own, Traditional regards them as inferior or even contemptible. He does not see his own way of life as a choice, and because he believes that there is only one right way to live, he sees no particular value in the fact of individuals' identification with ways of life other than his.

12 Ibid., p. 168; emphasis added.
13 Gray, *Isaiah Berlin*, pp. 160–161; see also George Crowder, "Pluralism and Liberalism," *Political Studies* 42 (1994): 297–299.

If value pluralism has objective validity, then Liberal knows something that Traditional does not. Otherwise put, Liberal is living her life under the aegis of truth, Traditional his under the canopy of illusion. What can be said about individuals can be predicated of societies whose constitutive principles are consistent with, or deny (implicitly or explicitly) the claims of, value pluralism. But truth or falsity in this matter is no small thing, because Liberal's epistemic superiority concerns one of the central questions of human existence. Surely, Weinstock concludes, this superiority is a compelling argument in Liberal's favor, and in favor of liberal societies.[14]

For current purposes, the limit of this otherwise compelling argument is that it does not take pluralism quite seriously enough. There are some genuine goods whose instantiation in ways of life allows or even requires illusion. (For example, it is impossible for contradictory religious creeds to be equally true, but many help undergird important individual and social virtues.) While self-aware value pluralists cannot lead such lives, they must recognize their value. To demand that every acceptable way of life reflect a conscious awareness of value pluralism is to affirm what value pluralism denies – the existence of a universally dominant value.

This does not mean that truth is no better than falsity, and it does not undercut the ability of value pluralism to make truth claims. But there is a distinction between the truth of a particular characterization of the domain of value and truth as a good within that domain. Weinstock's argument assumes that the truth (in the first sense) of value pluralism implies the dominant value of truth (in the second sense). But this conclusion does not follow logically, and human experience gives us good reasons for rejecting it.

So we must grant Gray this much: Value pluralism rules out any general appeal to the classic Enlightenment value of public truth as the ground for political liberalism. And we must also grant that we cannot move directly from the *inescapability* of choice to the *valuing* of choice that liberalism requires, a link Berlin too casually implies.

It is not difficult to fill the gap in Berlin's argument, however. The elaborated argument begins with the observation that every way of life represents a selection and ordering of values from a much wider field of possibilities. The process through which this particularization of value

14 Weinstock, "The Graying of Berlin," pp. 491–492.

takes place is what allows individuals and groups to become, and to find value in, what they are.

To be sure, this process does not always take the form of individual choice, and many forms of life do not give choice making an honored place. It is also true that from time to time, individuals and groups have chosen to create and live in these nonchoice societies. In so doing, they enjoy what I have called "expressive liberty" – a sense of identification with the organizing principles of a group or social order. In a wide range of circumstances, it would be wrong to intervene in such societies to compel them to recognize the authority of negative liberty over their own constitutive values.

These considerations do not suffice to reach Gray's conclusion, however, because they ignore the crucial question: What happens when (for whatever reason) certain individuals or subcommunities within a nonchoice society cease to feel this sense of identification, wish to lead their lives differently, perhaps wish to leave altogether? At this point, to the extent that the society enforces compliance or continued membership, it becomes, in Berlin's sense, a kind of prison.

Gray grasps the nettle firmly. There may, he says, be "worthwhile forms of life expressive of genuine human needs and embodying authentic varieties of human flourishing" whose survival depends on the denial of negative liberty. But why, he asks, should liberty always trump variety? "To claim that it must do so is to say that no form of life deserves to survive if it cannot withstand the force of the exercise of free choice by its members." This priority of liberty, he insists, is undercut by value pluralism.[15]

Gray's argument rests on a crucial ambiguity in the meaning of "worthwhile" as it applies to ways of life. There is a distinction between two strategies – call them "offensive" and "defensive" – for justifying a way of life. Offensive justification is addressed to those who are not (yet) leading that life. It is a proselytizing claim that it would be worthwhile for them to do so, a claim based on general propositions other than those they now embrace and, therefore, a claim they may well resist. Defensive justification, by contrast, is offered by or on behalf of people who are already leading a way of life. Its objective is not the creation or extension of a way of life but, rather, its protection against external pressure.

15 Gray, *Isaiah Berlin*, p. 152.

It is easy to see how defensive justification could be cast in particularist terms, along the following lines: "This is the way we have done things in the past, and we wish to continue doing so. Outsiders may see things differently, and that is their privilege – provided that they leave us alone." Gray is probably right to suggest that at least some traditional regimes seek to justify their arrangements in particularist rather than universalist terms. But by itself, this fact does not suffice to establish Gray's case, because particularist claims presuppose a high degree of social solidarity. To say that a way of life is collectively worthwhile is to say (in part) that it is worthwhile *for those who are actually leading it*. It is hard to see how that claim can be sustained unless the people in question identify (for whatever reason) with the way of life in question.[16] But if they do so, then the regime need not use coercion to maintain it. In these circumstances, the clash Gray depicts between individual choice and the collective preservation of a way of life should not arise.

At various junctures, Gray invokes Herder in support of the idea that political arrangements should help groups sustain their cultural identities.[17] Political pluralism, which gives neither liberal rights nor democratic self-government special status, leaves open the possibility that, for example, a constellation of state and market institutions could emerge in China that is legitimate "precisely because it owes little or nothing to Occidental ideologies and promotes the well-being of its subjects as that is perceived by them from the perspective of their indigenous cultural traditions."[18] An obvious difficulty with this expressivist view is that it cannot readily deal with the fact of political dissent. Substantial numbers of Chinese believe that their institutions should permit a significantly greater measure of individual freedom and democratic

---

16 In this regard, though not all others, I agree with the argument recently offered by Albert Dzur: "Liberals do not ask that all forms of life be justifiable to all persons, only that they be justifiable to the persons that live in them. Cultural options, practices, and traditions [that] only social groups can provide are important for individuals and may be inegalitarian.... Pluralists are wrong to suppose that... [liberal] political norms exclude the expression of inegalitarian and communitarian practices in society. What they do is prevent such practices from being imposed upon people without their proper endorsement" (Dzur, "Comprehensive Liberal Politics and the Fact of Pluralism," paper delivered at the 1998 Annual Meeting of the American Political Science Association, p. 10).

17 John Gray, *Enlightenment's Wake: Politics and Culture at the Close of the Modern Age* (London: Routledge, 1995), p. 136.

18 Ibid., p. 127.

self-government. Some appeal to Western norms in support of these views, while others ground their dissent in an interpretation of Chinese history and culture (emphasizing, for example, traditional critiques of official arrogance, unresponsiveness, and corruption). Although the Chinese democracy movement is a complex phenomenon, we can say with confidence that the cultural identity of its members is not accurately expressed by the current political status quo. Gray's deployment of the "indigenous" as a shield against external criticism elides the widespread, if not universal, facts of dissent within cultures and of the commingling of cultures. While the expressivist norm does possess substantial if not unrestricted moral force, it cannot rightly be used to immunize regimes against charges that they repress some of their citizens. Quite the reverse; cultural identity implies cultural identification. If I cease to identify with a given culture (or with the dominant interpretation of that culture), then political institutions that enforce a culture I now reject can hardly be said to express my identity.

While this argument is strong, its reach is limited. For example, it does not require the dominant forces in a society to alter institutions and policies so as to express the outlook of dissidents. It does mean that if a regime is unwilling to create an internal social space within which dissenters can enact their own conceptions of what gives meaning and worth to lives, then it must permit them to leave the regime in pursuit of alternative cultural contexts in which uncoerced expressive identification is possible. This sphere of cultural freedom need not be defined through rules of liberty pervading the entire society. It may take a range of forms, including constitutional guarantees of communal autonomy. But one thing is clear: Political communities cannot rightly be prisons, figuratively or literally.

This rejection of human imprisonment is the core of what Berlin means by negative liberty, and it is a principle with moral force across political boundaries. It extends to cultural communities within specific regimes as well. While value pluralism suggests that a wide range of family practices, including (say) arranged marriages, may be acceptable, cultural communities may not use their practices as instruments of imprisonment directed against members who have ceased to believe in them. So while a regime should not prohibit arranged marriages outright, it must be prepared to intervene if parents and community leaders

[margin note: what about indoctrinated children?]

use such coercive means as beating, starvation, and house arrest to force their decisions on unwilling young people.

The reach of this argument from cultural identification is limited in a second way: Identifying with (that is, accepting the constitutive values of) a way of life may not wholly obviate the need for coercion. It may be that the system of cooperation needed to sustain that way of life raises free-rider problems that can only be addressed through central mechanisms endowed with coercive power. But the point is this: If members of a group identify with a particular way of life, and if they come to understand that this way of life cannot be achieved without coercion, then they will endorse the creation of coercive institutions – in the name of promoting shared values.

This argument for coercion is very different from what would be needed to justify the imposition by some members of the society of their constitutive values on other members who disagree. Gray's position appears to rest on the premise that a way of life can be worthwhile even if some individuals and subcommunities leading that life do not experience it as worthwhile and can articulate their discontent in terms consistent with value pluralism. Indeed, that way of life may be worthwhile for the dominant groups that continue to identify with it. And the continued participation of the disaffected groups may be essential to the survival of the way of life, as slavery may be for forms of life that embody the not insignificant goods and virtues of aristocracy. But for the disaffected, the injunction "Remain loyal so that the way of life we find worthwhile can continue to exist" is unlikely to prove persuasive. Nor should it. Why should B agree to serve simply as a means to A's well-being? Nor, consistent with value pluralism, can dominant group A invoke paternalistic claims in favor of coercion, because by hypothesis there is no rational basis for judging subordinate group B's dissenting conception of a worthwhile way of life inferior to that of A.

If this argument is correct, then there is indeed a link between value pluralism and political liberalism. Value pluralism suggests that there is a range of indeterminacy within which various choices are rationally defensible, at least in the sense that they all fall above the Hampshire-Hart line of minimum decency. Because there is no single uniquely rational ordering or combination of such values, no one can provide a generally valid reason, binding on all individuals, for a particular ranking or combination. There is, therefore, no rational basis for restrictive policies whose justification includes the assertion that there is a unique rational ordering of value.[19] If value pluralism is correct, then as Steven Lukes puts it, "For the state to impose any single solution on some of its citizens is thus (not only from their standpoint) unreasonable."[20]

This argument draws its force from the underlying assumption that coercion always stands exposed to a potential demand for justification. Individuals and groups whose desires and values are thwarted by existing arrangements have an incentive to question those arrangements, and they are entitled to a reply. No one asks why it is legitimate for our movements to be influenced by gravity; they just are. But coercion is not a fact of nature, nor is it self-justifying. Just the reverse: There is a presumption against it, grounded in the pervasive human desire to go our own way in accordance with our own desires and beliefs. We may well disagree about the kinds of reasons that can rebut this presumption. But if someone responds to our demand to justify coercive arrangements with the claim that our understanding of the human good (including our own good) is radically defective, then value pluralists are bound to disagree in many (perhaps most) cases. The value-pluralist argument for negative liberty rests on the insufficiency of the reasons typically invoked in favor of restricting it. When the proffered reasons are sufficient, however, the burden shifts, and the failure of public institutions (or other individuals) to intervene in wrongful or self-destructive behavior may be judged morally culpable.[21]

This is not to say that there are no bases for state action other than a hierarchical ordering of conceptions of the good. While there may be no compelling reasons for driving on the right side of the road, rather than the left (or vice versa), there are compelling reasons to make a firm choice

19 This is not to say that all deliberative contexts (where the core question is what is to be done) are characterized by indeterminacy. While pluralism rules out simple priority rules, it permits deliberative closure made possible by the preponderance of relevant evidence and agreement in judgments concerning what is most urgent or important in given circumstances. On this distinction, see Isaiah Berlin and Bernard Williams, "Pluralism and Liberalism: A Reply," *Political Studies* 42 (1994): 306 307.

20 Steven Lukes, *Moral Conflict and Politics* (Oxford: Clarendon Press, 1991), p. 20.

21 For a more critical analysis of this argument from insufficient reason, see Glen Newey, "Metaphysics Postponed: Liberalism, Pluralism, and Neutrality," *Political Studies* 45 (1997), pp. 301–306. Newey's contention that value-pluralism does not warrant state neutrality is not on its face inconsistent with my claim that value-pluralism vindicates Berlin's understanding of negative liberty.

and to enforce it through law. An analogous logic is at work in the sphere of culture and morals. As George Crowder rightly observes, in practice, ways of life reflecting different orderings of value cannot always exist in the same social space. In such cases, the political system has no choice but to tilt in one direction or another.[22] But this unavoidable form of bias does not weaken the link between pluralism and liberalism. On the contrary, value pluralism itself teaches us that not all genuine goods can coexist in practice. Many political conflicts will reflect this fact. And when they do, it is not government arbitrarily restricting liberty but, rather, the structure of particular contexts of decision that necessarily limits the ability of some individuals to pursue ways of life that are fully defensible in theory.

Similar considerations are at work in what might be called the "diversity argument" connecting pluralism and political liberalism. Bernard Williams contends that "if there are many and competing genuine values, then the greater the extent to which a society tends to be single-valued, the more genuine values it neglects or suppresses. More, to this extent, must mean better."[23] Crowder's response is that the "deep multiplicity of human values . . . in itself gives us no reason to strive to accommodate, within a single society, as many of those values as possible."[24]

At this level of abstraction, anyway, Crowder appears to have the stronger argument. One can easily imagine societies that experience a narrowed range of values with greater intensity and more solidarity. Conversely, high-diversity societies may well pay a price in the form of weakened bonds among its members, attenuated trust, and a diminution of the distinctive pleasures of purposive collective action. From this perspective, it is not in principle irrational for societies weighing these costs and benefits to come down in favor of some limits to diversity.

But there is more to be said on this subject. On the theoretical plane, let me offer a modest proposition concerning what may be termed philosophical anthropology: While it is certainly true, as Gray and other critics of liberal universalism have argued, that we are beings whose good is radically underdetermined by our generic human nature, it is also the case that the diversity of human types is part of what exists prior to

---

22 George Crowder, "Pluralism and Liberalism," p. 297.
23 Bernard Williams, Introduction to Henry Hardy, ed., *Concepts and Categories: Philosophical Essays by Isaiah Berlin* (New York: Penguin Books, 1981), p. xvii.
24 Crowder, "Pluralism and Liberalism," p. 300.

cultural self-determination. This natural diversity means that narrow-valued societies (organized around dominant purposes, as Sparta was for war) will allow only a small fraction of their inhabitants to live their lives in a manner consistent with their flourishing and satisfaction. The rest will be pinched and stunted to some degree, and some ways of life will be ruled out altogether (no Socrates in Sparta). This is in principle undesirable, and best avoided if the cost of avoidance is not too high. To the maximum extent possible in human affairs, liberal societies avoid this stunting of human lives, no small element of their vindication as modes of political organization.[25]

One may object to this line of argument on the grounds that "human flourishing" is a principle outside of, and in conflict with, value pluralism. If this were so, Gray himself would be confused; his objection to liberalism is not that it deploys the bare concept of human flourishing but, rather, that "the range of forms of genuine human flourishing is considerably larger than can be accommodated within liberal forms of life."[26] But Gray is not confused on this point. Value pluralists believe that there is a wide range of ways in which human beings can flourish, but not that there is no distinction between developed and stunted lives, or no reason to prefer development to stunting. Children who grow up without attachments to parents and peers, in circumstances of pervasive physical insecurity, disconnected from all potential sources of meaning and purpose in their lives, have been harmed, from the standpoint not of some, but rather all, viable conceptions of flourishing.[27]

25 In fairness, I should note that in his most recent publication, Crowder has come around to the view that there is a valid general argument connecting pluralism to liberalism via the value of diversity. He distinguishes this argument from the kind of contingent or contextual argument for liberalism in specific modern circumstances that Gray is prepared to acknowledge (Crowder, "From Value Pluralism to Liberalism," *Critical Review of International Social and Political Philosophy* 1, 3 [1998]: 2–17).

26 Gray, *Enlightenment's Wake*, p. 133.

27 This is an extension of an argument made by Brian Barry to the effect that societies with wildly divergent affirmative conceptions of moral and cultural goods nonetheless agree negatively on what constitutes "harm." So, for example, societies use very similar strategies for the legal infliction of punishment: deprivation of liberty and property, among others [Barry, *A Treatise on Social Justice*, Volume 1: *Theories of Justice* (Berkeley: University of California Press, 1989), pp. 141–142.]. And while societies disagree about the moral acceptability of other kinds of punishment – the infliction of physical pain, mutilation, and death, for example – the disagreement takes place in the context of agreement that these disputed forms of punishment constitute harm, that is, the deprivation of human goods.

There is a more practical (or perhaps historical) argument as well that connects value pluralism to political liberalism. Liberty unleashes diversity in ways that are difficult to reverse. It is one thing for narrow societies to try to hold the line against the forces of diversification (for example, by limiting the sources of information that are allowed to enter), quite another for them to try to squelch diversity once it has taken hold and is instantiated in the life and consciousness of individuals or groups within those societies. Here we must, I think, agree with Pratap Mehta: Diversity, dissent, and demands for reasonable justifications of social arrangements are no longer confined to the West but are ubiquitous, even in societies where those arrangements may have long been taken for granted. The costs of repression have soared and continue to rise. A minimally decent response to these conditions will require institutions and practices far closer to liberal democracy than to autocracy.[28] The shift Gray advocates from philosophical to historical arguments for liberal democracy thus may prove less inhospitable to universalist claims than he supposes.

Michael Walzer suggests that the philosophical and historical considerations connecting value pluralism and political liberalism may be less important than the common fundamental orientation that gives rise to both:

I don't know anyone who believes in value pluralism who isn't a liberal, in sensibility as well as conviction. . . . You have to look at the world in a receptive and generous way to see a pluralism of Berlin's sort. . . . And you also have to look at the world in a skeptical way, since the adherents of of each of the different values are likely to rank them very high on a scale designed for just that purpose. And receptivity, generosity, and skepticism are, if not liberal values, then qualities of mind that make it possible to accept liberal values (or better, that make it likely that liberal values will be accepted).[29]

One may wonder whether these qualities of mind systematically characterize liberals, many of whom are decidedly ungenerous when faced with traditional ways of life they regard as stultifying and benighted. But clearly, a politics conducted in full awareness of value pluralism will find it impossible to pick out, or to promote, a single way of life as

28 Pratap Mehta, "Pluralism After Liberalism?" *Critical Review* 11, 4 (1997): 513–515.
29 Michael Walzer, "Are There Limits to Liberalism?" *New York Review of Books*, October 19, 1995, p. 31.

simply best for everyone, everywhere, at all times. It will be receptive to a wide though not unlimited range of value-based claims. It will be generous to ways of life reflecting unusual but not indefensible choices among, or orderings of, basic values. And it will be intensely skeptical in the face of claims that way of life A is clearly preferable to B and therefore deserves political support, or that C is simply intolerable and merits forcible suppression.

This politics of self-aware pluralism will be a different kind of liberalism, however. The value-pluralist liberal state will respect self-aware, autonomous lives but will not insist on promoting Socratic or Millian ideals (or any others) as valid for all citizens. It will limit the agreement on principles and practices required of all citizens to constitutional essentials, parsimoniously understood. It will seek to create conditions within which, to the greatest extent possible, individuals and groups can lead their lives in accordance with their own understanding of what gives life meaning and purpose. And it will vigorously defend the ability of individuals to exit from ways of life with which they have ceased to identify. It is, in short, a liberalism that takes seriously both Berlin's claim that imprisonment is the essence of unfreedom and his generous receptivity to understandings of human existence that do not give pride of place to liberty.

LIBERAL UNIVERSALISM AND POLITICAL PRUDENCE

To offer, as I have, a qualified defense of liberal universalism in the context of value pluralism is not in any way to recommend the imposition of liberal institutions everywhere. Gray's argument is motivated as much by opposition to post–Cold War triumphalism as by theoretical considerations.[30] He is surely right to emphasize the need for political flexibility and to suggest that differences of national history, culture, and economic circumstances should influence judgments about what should be done here and now. Value pluralism sensitizes us to the possibility that in dire circumstances, even the most basic constituents of decent human lives may come into conflict. If political authorities have used repression to keep the lid on ethnic and religious tensions, a pell-mell move to liberal institutions may unleash communal strife. Increasing

30 Gray, *Enlightenment's Wake,* Chapters 5 and 9.

the role of markets may well prove counterproductive in the absence of transparency, a social safety net, and the appropriate legal-institutional framework. In the absence of elementary order and security, no progress is possible, but the means needed to secure order in badly injured societies may violate otherwise desirable public norms.

The conclusions of liberal ideal theory, whatever they may be, are manifestly inadequate as blueprints for practical policy making in the post–Cold War world. In some circumstances (South Africa, for example), the best response to ethnic strife may be constitution making that emphasizes federalism and communal guarantees; in other circumstances, it may be necessary to undertake the division of a multiethnic state into a multiplicity of states, each with a dominant ethnic group; in still other circumstances, where groups are geographically intermingled and cannot be disentangled, strengthened central state institutions capable of using the threat of coercion to keep the peace may be the best anyone can do.

Liberal pluralists can accept all the requirements of political prudence operating in highly imperfect circumstances, although they may wonder whether Gray's blanket invocation of the need for politics really gets us very far.[31] What they cannot accept is Gray's proposal that some combination of Hobbesian peace and Herderian cultural expression constitutes an adequate account of public morality.[32]

There are three reasons for this refusal. The first is conceptual: As we have seen, liberal pluralists affirm what Gray denies, that value pluralism is consistent with, and lends support to, negative liberty understood in Berlin's fashion as the opposite of imprisonment. The second reason is empirical: Liberal pluralists believe that disastrous violations of what Gray himself acknowledges as the essential elements of human decency are far less likely to occur in regimes with freedom of the press and governing institutions responsive to the people.

The third and deepest reason that liberal pluralists cannot accept Gray's Hobbesian/Herderian politics rests on their understanding of human nature and culture. They readily acknowledge that not all societies are or need be well disposed toward the preference for individual choice characteristic of advanced industrial societies, especially those of

31 For an elaboration of these doubts, see Ira Katznelson, "A Properly Defended Liberalism: On John Gray and the Filling of Political Life," *Social Research* 61, 3 (1994): 624–628.
32 Gray, *Enlightenment's Wake*, p. 140.

the English-speaking world. But they nonetheless believe that most human beings bridle at repressive policies and resist them when they can. While liberal pluralists celebrate legitimate diversity among cultures, they suspect that diversity will almost always exist within cultures as well and that a culture's smoothly homogeneous public face reflects the covert operation of power. For these reasons, among others, liberal pluralists think it necessary and proper to advocate institutions that thwart oppression, wherever it may occur. Gray rightly suggests that "at least some non-liberal regimes and cultural forms possess genuine virtues and harbour authentic excellences that are weak, or lacking, in liberal regimes."[33] While liberal pluralists agree, they think it necessary to pay attention as well to the individuals and groups residing within these nonliberal contexts who fail to identify with their dominant norms.[34] It is not clear that this concern will decisively weaken nonliberal virtues and excellences. But when it does, we have good reason to doubt that the nonliberal regime ever conformed to the Herderian model of cultural expressiveness.

33 Ibid., p. 86.
34 See especially Richard E. Flathman, "From Unicity to Plurality and On to Singularity," *Social Research* 61, 3 (1994): 671–686.

6

VALUE PLURALISM AND POLITICAL COMMUNITY

Even though value pluralism is not relativism, it certainly embodies what Thomas Nagel has called the fragmentation of value.[1] But political order cannot be maintained without some agreement. It is not unreasonable to fear that once value pluralism is publicly acknowledged as legitimate, it may unleash centrifugal forces that make a decently ordered public life impossible. Within the pluralist framework, how is the basis for a viable political community to be secured?

In this chapter I explore three kinds of responses to this question: the requirements of public order; the structuring processes of constitutionalism; and the force of ethical presumptions.

THE MINIMUM CONDITIONS OF PUBLIC ORDER

While pluralists cannot regard social peace and stability as dominant goods in all circumstances, they recognize that these goods typically help create the framework within which the attainment of other goods becomes possible. They recognize, then, that anarchy is the enemy of pluralism and that political community is (within limits) its friend. Pluralists must therefore endorse what I shall call the minimum conditions of public order.

For modern societies these conditions form a familiar list. Among them are clear and stable property relations, the rule of law, a public authority with the capacity to enforce the law, an economy that does not divide the population permanently between a thin stratum of the rich and the numerous poor, and a sense of membership in the political

[1] Thomas Nagel, "The Fragmentation of Value," in *Mortal Questions* (Cambridge: Cambridge University Press, 1979).

community strong enough (in most circumstances, anyway) to override ethnic and religious differences.

It follows that pluralists are also committed to what may be called the conditions of the conditions – that is, those economic and social processes that experience suggests are needed (at least in modern and modernizing societies) to secure the minimum conditions of public order. Among these are a suitably regulated market economy, a basic level of social provision, and a system of education sufficient to promote not only economic competence but also law-abidingness and civic attachment.

I do not mean to suggest that this public framework constitutes an ensemble of goods and values that always outweighs other goods and values. Under unusual circumstances the moral costs of public life may become too high to be endured, and individuals may feel impelled toward conscientious objection or outright resistance. Nonetheless, pluralists will understand that in the vast majority of circumstances, reliable public order increases, rather than undermines, the ability of individuals to live in accordance with their own conceptions of what gives life meaning and value. This does not mean that each can live out his or her conception to the hilt. The ensemble of conditions of public order will typically require some modification of each individual's primary desires. In the absence of public order, however, the threat to those desires will almost always be much greater. It is rational and reasonable, therefore, for pluralists to incorporate a shared sense of the minimum conditions of public order into the ensemble of goods they value and pursue.

CONSTITUTIONALISM

Constitutionalism offers a second kind of response to the challenge posed by the centrifugal tendencies of moral pluralism. Beyond the common foundation and requisites of public order, every political community assumes a distinctive form and identity through its constitution. A constitution, we may say, represents an authoritative partial ordering of public values. It selects a subset of worthy values, brings them to the foreground, and subordinates others to them. These preferred values then become the benchmarks for assessing legislation, public policy, and even the condition of public culture. Various aspects of this definition require further elaboration.

Within the pluralist understanding, to begin, there is no single constitutional ordering that is rationally preferable to all others – certainly not across differences of space, time, and culture, and arguably not even within a given situation. Nonetheless, the worth of a constitution can be assessed along three dimensions: Call them realism, coherence, and congruence. A constitution is realistic if the demands it places on citizens are not too heavy for them to bear. A constitution is coherent if the ensemble of values it represents are not too diverse to coexist within the same community. A constitution is congruent if its broad outlines correspond to the moral sentiments of the community and to the situation that community confronts.

Nor, for the pluralist, is there a single account of how a given constitution comes to be authoritative. One model is covenantal acceptance: the people of Israel at Sinai. Another is public ratification of the work of a constitutional convention, as in the United States. A third is bargaining among representatives of large forces in a divided society – the process that led to the post-apartheid South African constitution, for example. A fourth flows from the ability of a great leader to express the spirit of the needs of a people in a practicable manner – the Napoleonic Code, or the French Fifth Republic. It is even possible for a conqueror to establish an authoritative constitution for a conquered people, as the Allies did for Germany (and the United States for Japan) after World War II.

Authoritativeness, we may say, has two sorts of necessary conditions – the objective and the subjective. No proposed constitution can become authoritative if it falls below the minimum requirements of realism, coherence, and congruence. Nor can it be authoritative if it fails to gain broad acceptance within the community – perhaps not immediately, but within a reasonable period of time. While the post–World War II German constitution met this condition, it seems clear in retrospect that the post–World War I Weimar Republic never did.

A constitution represents only a "partial ordering" of value in three senses. In the first place, there is no guarantee that a community's distinctive constitutional values will always be consistent with the minimum requirements of public order, or that in cases of conflict, public order must yield to constitutional values. Second, it is not the case that constitutional values will always dominate an individual's ensemble of personal values. There are circumstances in which it is not unreasonable for individuals to place the values at the core of their identity above the requirements of citizenship.

Third, a constitution is only a partial ordering because the plurality of values that it establishes as preferred will unavoidably come into conflict with one another. Such conflicts are a familiar feature of U.S. constitutionalism. Public purposes understood in the consequentialist manner ("domestic tranquility") may clash with individual rights understood deontologically (a "fair trial"). And individual rights may themselves come into conflict; consider the tension between the right to a fair trial and freedom of the press.

From a pluralist standpoint, it is inevitable that many of these conflicts will have no single rationally compelling solution. Reasonable men and women may well disagree about the relative weight to be attached to competing values, and many will be able to make legitimate appeal to different features of the constitutional framework. There are no strict lexical orderings, even in theory, among basic values.

In Federalist #51, James Madison poses a famous rhetorical question: "[W]hat is government itself but the greatest of all reflections on human nature?" And he continues: "If men were angels, no government would be necessary." A philosophical pluralist must disagree. Even if every individual were in Madison's sense angelic – perfectly capable of subordinating ambition and self-interest to reason and public spirit – nonetheless, the incapacity of human reason to resolve fully many clashes among worthy values means that authoritative mechanisms for resolving disputes remain indispensable. The more reasonable individuals are, the more clearly they will understand the need for such mechanisms. And this is true even if there is broad public consensus on constitutional matters – that is, on the ensemble of values that are to be brought into the foreground.

From a pluralist standpoint, individuals vested with the power to make authoritative decisions – whether judicial, legislative, or executive – must understand that many of the controversies they are called on to resolve represent the clash not of good and bad but, rather, of good and good. This means that these individuals must carry out their duties in a particular spirit: To the maximum extent feasible, their decisions should reflect what is valuable, not only to the winners but also to the losers. Sometimes this will not be possible. But when not required by the logic of the matter to be resolved, winner-take-all decisions needlessly (and therefore wrongfully) diverge from the balance of underlying values at stake.

ETHICAL PRESUMPTION

The third way in which the centrifugal tendencies of moral pluralism are moderated is through a structure of relationships between values that I shall call ethical presumption. To understand the nature of presumption, we must start farther back.

More than three decades ago, the noted student of jurisprudence Chaim Perelman observed that few philosophers have explored analogies between philosophy and law. Starting with Plato, many have suggested parallels between philosophy and mathematics. More recently, others have tried to refashion philosophy along the lines of natural science. But important structural similarities between philosophy and law have been neglected, Perelman suggests.[2]

In law, reasonable and honest people can reach differing conclusions (unlike in mathematics) such that additional evidence cannot suffice to overcome their differences (unlike in the sciences). The ubiquity of reasonable disagreement in the law suggests a conception of rational decision that is neither determined by truth nor driven by arbitrary will, and it makes necessary structures of decision that can give authoritative force to one reasonable view over others. Indeed, Perelman argues, the very coherence of the idea of authority rests on this conception of decisions that are consistent with but not required by reason. Authority is superfluous, or at best derivative, in spheres in which reason compels a unique result.[3]

Perelman's account of reasonable disagreement is more than a little reminiscent of Aristotle's discussion of deliberation. Aristotle begins, and proceeds, by enumerating the matters about which we do not deliberate: mathematical truths, law-governed regularities of nature, matters of chance, or particular facts, among others. Instead, we deliberate about matters of human agency in which actions do not generate fully predictable results, matters which "though subject to rules that generally

2 "What the Philosopher May Learn from the Study of Law," in Chaim Perelman, *Justice* (New York: Random House, 1967), pp. 91–110.
3 Ibid., p. 107.

hold good, are uncertain in their issue."[4] So deliberation is the effort to choose the best course, all things considered, in circumstances in which reason shapes but does not fully determine that course.

Perelman takes Aristotle's argument one important step farther. The nature of law, and of practical deliberation more generally, points toward the necessary ground of human freedom:

> Only the existence of an argumentation that is neither compelling nor arbitrary can give meaning to human freedom, a state in which a reasonable choice can be exercised. If freedom was no more than necessary adherence to a previously given natural order, it would exclude all possibility of choice; and if the exercise of freedom were not based on reasons, every choice would be irrational and would be reduced to an arbitrary decision operating in an intellectual void.[5]

In short, neither Spinoza's determinism nor Sartre's decisionism can explain human freedom as we experience and practice it. Freedom operates in a zone of partial but not complete regularity, a discursive arena in which some reasons are better than others but none is clearly dominant over all the rest in every situation. If ethics and politics are part of this zone, as they evidently are, then their substance will reflect this ceaseless interplay of strong but not compelling reasons for grappling with the variability of practical circumstances.

Perelman observes that every system of law embodies a presumption in favor of past decisions. The new and the old do not have to be treated in the same fashion; law teaches us to abandon existing rules only if good reasons justify their replacement. This presumption is not absolute, but the burden of proof falls on those advocating change.[6] In a similar spirit, the nineteenth-century scholar Richard Whately, one of the founders of the modern study of argumentation, contended that while the majority of existing institutions and practices are susceptible

---

4 *Nicomachean Ethics* III. iii. 1112b–1113a. For an outstanding discussion of Aristotelian deliberation influenced by value pluralism, see David Wiggins, "Deliberation and Practical Reason," in Joseph Raz, ed., *Practical Reasoning* (Oxford: Oxford University Press, 1978), pp. 144–152.

5 Quoted in Richard H. Gaskins, *Burdens of Proof in Modern Discourse* (New Haven, Conn.: Yale University Press, 1992), p. 31.

6 Perelman, "What the Philosopher May Learn from the Study of Law," p. 104. See also Chaim Perelman and L. Olbrechts-Tyteca, *The New Rhetoric: A Treatise on Argumentation*, trans. John Wilkinson and Purcell Weaver (Notre Dame, Ind.: University of Notre Dame Press, 1969), section 17 ("Presumptions").

of improvement, nonetheless "the 'Burden of Proof' lies with him who proposes an alteration; simply, on the ground that since a change is not a good in itself, he who demands a change should show cause for it."[7]

The reasoning underlying this stance is straightforward. The merits and defects of the status quo are well known. Unless the status quo is so intolerable that any change would be for the better, or at least not for the worse, then there is a possibility that a proposed change could produce a state of affairs that is even less desirable than the admittedly defective status quo. That is why the burden of proof is on the advocate of change to show why the proposed reform is unlikely to make matters worse, all things considered, and that those at greatest risk of harm are situated well enough to take a hit without suffering a devastating loss that no one would reasonably accept.

The phenomenon of legal presumption has a broader philosophical implication, Perelman suggests. Specifically, the Cartesian prescription for universal doubt makes no sense:

What normal man would put any of his convictions into doubt if the reasons for doubt were not more solid than the opinion to which they were opposed? To shake a belief there is need, as with a lever, for a point of leverage more solid than what is to be moved.... One could formulate the principle of inertia as a directive: One should not change anything without reason. If one maintains that our ideas, our rules, and our behavior are devoid of an absolute foundation, and that for this reason, the pros and cons are equally worthy, and that one must therefore in philosophy make a tabula rasa of our past, one expresses an exigency that comes from utopia and to which one can only conform fictitiously.[8]

Whether or not universal doubt is a feasible strategy for theoretical philosophy (and many follow Perelman in arguing that it is not), it is notable that Descartes does not extend it (or the quest for certainty) to practical life. He distinguishes (in Perelman's formulation) between "our ideas" and "our behavior." This suggests an important distinction between theoretical and practical reflection. The decision to accept no merely probable metaphysical or scientific proposition as true may leave the mind suspended in a state of permanent agnosticism. The

---

7 Richard Whately, *Elements of Rhetoric*, intr. Charlotte Downey and Howard Coughlin (Delmar, N.Y.: Scholars' Facsimiles and Reprints, 1991), p. 91.

8 Perelman, "What the Philosopher May Learn from the Study of Law," pp. 102–103.

consequences for practice are very different: The decision to accept no merely probable moral or political proposition as valid calls the status quo into question without being able to put anything in its place. But practical life does not wait for ethics and political philosophy to arrive at certainty. Decisions must be made, here and now, on the basis of limited (or complex and confusing) evidence and argument. The practical analogue of theoretical agnosticism – namely, indecision that leads to inaction – is itself a decision that affects (usually but not always sustains) the status quo.[9] While the presumption in favor of the status quo may appear conservative, the willingness to make practical decisions on grounds well short of certainty opens the door to changes that a more stringent standard would rule out.

The reasons advanced to justify decisions typically include general maxims tacitly (or less frequently explicitly) derived from moral or political theory. The absence of certainty is not confined to the empirical dimensions of decision making but reflects its normative dimensions as well. In this respect, among others, Perelman's suggestion that philosophy could fruitfully take its bearings from law seems plausible, at least for practical philosophy. This is why moral and political philosophy may have something to learn from the role presumptions play in jurisprudence.

In an important article, Judge J. Harvie Wilkinson III elaborates the conception of presumption in a legal context. As a backdrop, he sketches two opposed pure notions of judging: strict adherence to rules, without exception, and equity-based jurisprudence that takes its bearings from the facts of each case. The problem with strict rules is that they will inevitably run up against exceptional cases in which their application will appear harsh and unreasonable. The problem with unfettered equity is that it provides little predictability or uniformity, diluting the principal advantages of the rule of law.[10] (For purposes of this discussion, I will follow Wilkinson in presupposing that the result or meaning of applying rules to particular cases is not in doubt. The frequent uncertainty of interpreting rules raises other questions that I want to set aside for now.)

9 For discussion on this point, see Douglas Walton, *Arguments from Ignorance* (University Park: Pennsylvania State University Press, 1996), pp. 214–217.
10 J. Harvie Wilkinson III, "Toward a Jurisprudence of Presumptions," *New York University Law Review* 67 (1992): 908–910.

Against this backdrop, the jurisprudence of presumptions emerges as an attempt to combine the advantages of rules – clarity, predictability, uniformity – with those of flexibility, prudence, and common sense. The strength of a legal presumption, Wilkinson declares, lies in its rootedness in the rule of law; its vulnerability lies in the inability of the drafter of any legal rule to anticipate all the factual circumstances to which it may be applicable.[11]

In a famous discussion, Aristotle suggests that this combination of strength and vulnerability is inherent in the nature of law and law making itself:

Law is always a general statement, yet there are cases which it is not possible to cover in a general statement. In matters therefore where, while it is necessary to speak in general terms, it is not possible to do so correctly, the law takes into consideration the majority of cases, although it is not unaware of the error this involves. And this does not make it a wrong law; for the error is not in the law nor in the lawgiver, but in the nature of the case: the material of conduct is essentially irregular. When therefore the law lays down a general rule, and thereafter a case arises which is an exception to the rule, it is then right, where the lawgiver's pronouncement because of its absoluteness is defective and erroneous, to rectify the defect by deciding as the lawgiver would himself decide if he were present on the occasion, and would have enacted if he had been cognizant of the case in question.[12]

Because the tension between generality and particularity is inherent in the nature of law, there are, Wilkinson suggests, no exceptionless absolute principles in law. Those that may appear absolute are in fact strong presumptions that may be overcome in specific circumstances. Not that rebutting a strong presumption is easy; one may understand it as a well-defended fortress that would require a powerful assault to conquer. Some presumptions are stronger than others. In American constitutional law, the presumption in favor of free political speech can be overcome only by the most compelling public interest; in criminal cases, the presumption of innocence can be overcome only by evidence of guilt beyond a reasonable doubt, a difficult standard to meet. The burden of proof in civil cases is less stringent; the preponderance (that is, the greater part) of the evidence is required to sustain the plaintiff's claim.

11 Ibid., p. 908.
12 *Nicomachean Ethics* V. x. 1137b.

In part, the variation among standards governing the burden of proof in different categories of cases reflects differences among the goods and values at stake. In criminal cases, for example, individuals' lives and liberty are at stake. The prosecution's burden of proof beyond a reasonable doubt is designed to minimize the chances that individuals will be wrongfully deprived of these very great goods, which enjoy the status of natural as well as civil rights in American civic philosophy. The system cannot wholly eliminate the possibility of such wrongful deprivation, however. The only way to do so is never to convict anyone of a felony, which would deprive the entire society of the advantages of the rule of law. In a universe of plural and competing goods, highly demanding protections for accused persons may impose excessive costs along other key dimensions of public value.

We can go farther, Wilkinson suggests, toward a precise account of how the jurisprudence of presumptions operates in practice. First, the adjudicator must identify the relevant rule of law. Second, the "presumptive strength" of that rule must be identified. As we have seen, some rules enjoy a preferred position in our constitutional system, while others are secondary or tertiary. Third, the adjudicator must assess the "degree of stress" that an unforeseen circumstance imposes on that rule. In the case of political speech, for example, not only must the countervailing state interest be powerful as a matter of principle, but the facts of the particular case must clearly bring that interest into play. Fourth, the adjudicator must specify, so far as possible, the costs of departing from the rule laid down, including not only the costs in the particular case but the longer-term damage to the credibility of the rule itself. Finally, the decision maker must explain why the result achieved by making an exception to the rule is preferable, all things considered, to following the rule.[13]

I want to underscore two features of this schema. First, it does not identify some neutral point of equipoise between the jurisprudence of rules and the jurisprudence of equity. Legal rules enjoy a status very different from that of (say) propositions advanced in a dialogue. If laid down by those duly empowered to create them, the rules have presumptive authority flowing from their source. There is a presumption – stronger in some cases than others, but always powerful – in favor of applying the rules laid down. The burden of proof lies on those who

13 Wilkinson, "Toward a Jurisprudence of Presumptions," p. 914.

74

would relax the rules or carve out exceptions to them. In these circumstances, it would not suffice to show that making an accommodation would yield an outcome just as good, all things considered, as following the rule. A preponderance of considerations must point toward the exception being sought. (Just how strong a preponderance will depend on the nature of the rule in question.)

Second, the process of justifying the exception often takes place in a context of multiple values. The rule in question, let us say, seeks to promote a particular public value. The case for granting an exception will typically appeal to a different value; if allowed to operate without modification in pursuit of its intended value, it may be alleged, the rule will exact too high a price as measured along another important dimension of value that the system of law cannot reasonably ignore.

I began this discussion of legal presumptions with Perelman's suggestion that philosophy should take its bearings from law and jurisprudence. I now want to apply this suggestion to the special case of practical – that is, moral and political – philosophy. My hypothesis is this: Like legal rules, moral and political principles act as rebuttable presumptions. The more entrenched the principle, the more central it is to our understanding, the weightier the considerations that will be needed to override it. But no principle is absolute, that is, exceptionless.[14] Two examples from applied ethics will clarify this conjecture.

Sissela Bok's analysis of lying takes its bearings from a "presumption against lying" – the premise that

[t]ruthful statements are preferable to lies in the absence of special considerations. This premise gives an initial negative weight to lies. It holds that they are not neutral from the point of view of our choices; that lying requires explanation, whereas truth ordinarily does not.[15]

Bok explores, but ultimately rejects, the thesis that one should never lie; in certain extreme but hardly unknown situations, the consequences of truth-telling are simply unacceptable (see her Chapter 3). The inquiry then turns to the nature of valid excuses – considerations of value

14 For a clear discussion of the comparative strength of arguments, see Joseph Raz, *Practical Reason and Norms* (London: Hutchinson, 1975), pp. 25–28. See also Perelman and Olbrechts-Tyteca, *The New Rhetoric*, section 98.
15 Sissela Bok, *Lying: Moral Choice in Public and Private Life*, with a new preface (New York: Vintage, 1999), p. 30.

sufficient to rebut the presumption against lying. Grotius offers one important argument, that in some circumstances an agent bent on doing evil forfeits his right to truth. For example, you are not morally obligated to tell the truth when the secret police of a tyrannical regime ask whether you are harboring refugees from persecution.[16] Another important suggestion is that in circumstances in which it is justified to use force in self-defense or to protect innocent third parties, it would also be acceptable to use forms of deceit, including lies.[17] There are several other categories of excuses that are potentially valid in specific circumstances. Nonetheless, the presumption in favor of truth-telling remains powerful, and the grounds for rebutting that presumption remain stringent.

Michael Walzer's exploration of just and unjust wars deploys the classic distinction between the justice of war – the valid or invalid reasons for which wars are fought – and justice in war – the permissible or forbidden means by which wars are conducted. Justice in war is delimited by what Walzer calls the war convention. At the heart of that convention is a sharp distinction between combatants and noncombatants. The latter are "men and women with rights [who] cannot be used for some military purpose, even if it is a legitimate purpose."[18] Even just wars must be fought justly; the ends of wars do not suffice to justify the means of war.

Or do they? In the end, Walzer cannot quite defend the thesis that the rights of noncombatants are inviolate, regardless of the circumstances. While he resists utilitarianism, theories of proportionality, and even sliding-scale justifications of means relative to the justice of ends as insufficiently stringent, the weight of human experience moves him to offer instead a thesis that falls just short of absolutism: Instead of *fiat justicia ruat coelum,* act justly unless the heavens are *really* about to fall.[19] The war convention is overriden in cases of imminent catastrophe or supreme emergency – credible threats to the very existence of a nation or a people, or the likely victory of a murderous tyranny.[20]

From this perspective, if the terror bombing of German cities during World War II had been absolutely necessary to defeat Hitler, it would

16 Ibid., p. 32.
17 Ibid., p. 41.
18 Michael Walzer, *Just and Unjust Wars,* 3d ed. (New York: Basic Books, 2000), p. 137.
19 Ibid., p. 231.
20 Ibid., p. 232.

have been justified. Similarly (this is my example, not Walzer's), if the Israelis were faced with imminent defeat and probable genocide at the hands of Arab military forces, they would be justified in using atomic weapons against Damascus and Baghdad if there were no other way of averting catastrophe. Rights have great moral weight, but they do not function as trumps in every shuffle of the deck. Rights have enormous value, but they are not the only things of value in our moral universe.

The maxim that practical principles function as powerful but rebuttable presumptions applies to two arenas that are important for our purposes. The first may be called ordinary universal morality – the principles of conduct that are embedded in different forms in the world's great religions and in the normal social practices of humankind. Strictures against lying, theft, murder, sexual anarchy, and the oppression of the weak, among many others, constitute this realm.

The maxim of practical principles as presumptions also applies, less obviously, to the arena of public culture, by which I mean the ensemble of practical principles that gives each political community its distinct identity. In the case of the United States, for example, a kind of social egalitarianism, libertarianism, commitment to equal opportunity and personal responsibility, and mistrust of authority (including governmental authority) helps define a public culture that differs from that of other democratic nations. The wind is in the sails of those who deploy these principles in defense of specific public policy proposals. By contrast, those who employ opposed principles (say, sociological determinism, rather than personal responsibility) bear a heavy burden of proof.

I do not want to be misunderstood as suggesting that principles of public culture are immune to skeptical questioning. On the contrary, skeptics have a number of dialectical tools ready at hand. The skeptic may suggest, first, that there are cases in which it makes no sense to apply the dominant principles. For example, do we really want to attribute personal responsibility to someone laboring under a severe cognitive distortion? Second, the skeptic may suggest that the public culture is incoherent, that some of its principles contradict others when applied to particular cases, and that in regard to such cases, we have no choice but to think for ourselves. Third, the skeptic may suggest that the strict application of a particular principle will lead to results that a morally decent person of common sense would find hard to accept. This possibility reflects the fact that a particular public culture always functions in relation to, and sometimes stands in tension with, the background code of universal ordinary morality.

Let us now return to our point of departure. It is not unreasonable to fear that pluralism's dispersion of value makes the maintenance of political community difficult at best. In response, we have explored three sources of commonality that are consistent with pluralism: the minimum demands of public order; constitutionalism understood as the selection of preferred goods and values; and the ethical presumptions both of universal ordinary morality and of specific public cultures. Taken together, these sources ask each individual to consider what it means to be a member of the human species, to be an individual whose conception of a good and valuable life can only be realized within the framework of public order, and to be a social being embedded in, though not determined by, a specific constitution and public culture. The political meaning of moral pluralism emerges in the unending dialogue between the differentiating force of individuality and the organizing tendencies of commonality.

PART III

THE PRACTICE OF LIBERAL PLURALISM

7

DEMOCRACY AND VALUE PLURALISM

INTRODUCTION

My overall thesis in exploring the relationship between democracy and value pluralism is this: If there are good reasons to take value pluralism seriously, then it becomes more difficult to accord democracy the unquestioned normative priority it typically enjoys in both ordinary and philosophical discourse. Not only is the scope of democratic political authority restricted; certain alternatives to democracy within the sphere of politics must be taken more seriously than they usually are.

This may appear a strange venture. For many (theorists and citizens alike), the standing of democracy is, like slavery, a settled question. What good can be done by reopening it? Surely twentieth-century experience has taught us that democracy is preferable to any other mode of government. If theory raises doubts about democratic practice, so much the worse for theory.

It is not my intention to mount an assault on democracy. But I do want to suggest that when democracy overreaches, other important values can be imperiled. I also want to suggest that more careful attention to political experience (including our own) yields a more nuanced account of the types of governance we find justifiable in practice.

As a logical matter, the broad implication of value pluralism is clear. If there are no overriding values, then democracy cannot be such a value. If it is not, then statements of the form "X promotes (or sustains, or is most consistent with) democracy" are not sufficient to warrant the conclusion that "X is, all things considered, what we should do."

The question is whether in the real world there are any significant concrete phenomena that correspond to this logical abstraction. I think there are, in two categories: limits on the reach of politics, including democratic politics; and alternatives to democracy within the political sphere.

THE LIMITS OF POLITICS

Democracy is an ordering of the political domain. It is possible but not easy to contend that politics is coextensive with the totality of human endeavors and concerns. If, as seems more plausible, politics is not the totality of human life, and if pluralism is correct, political goods – including democracy – cannot always be overriding. From a pluralist perspective, in specific circumstances it will be possible to say, "X is a procedurally correct determination of a democratic polity, but nonetheless I (a citizen of that polity) have compelling reasons not to do X but something else instead." Two such reasons are truth and liberty.

Truth

Consider the nature of democratic authority over scientific inquiry. It seems perfectly appropriate for democratic institutions to determine (e.g.) the distribution of resources devoted to various domains of inquiry. From the standpoint of many physicists, it may be regrettable when a democratic government decides not to invest the billions of dollars needed to construct the next generation of particle accelerators, but it cannot be said that the government has overstepped its bounds. It is legitimate, moreover, for democratic governments to make such decisions based, in part, on their assessment of the kinds of inquiry that are most likely to sustain democratic institutions. Democracies can impose restrictions on allowable research methods (on human subjects, for example), although these restraints may make it more difficult for research to succeed. And in certain circumstances, it may even be legitimate and appropriate for democracies to restrict the public discussion of specific research results.

Distinct from all these actions is direct government intervention to determine the outcome of inquiry. The quest for truth is an autonomous activity guided by its own rules. To be sure, communities of inquiry shape those rules and judge their products, but not on a democratic basis.

One of the sorriest episodes in the history of the Soviet Union was the use of state power to impose the pseudo-Lamarckian views of the quack agronomist Trofim Lysenko on the whole of Soviet biology. Plant scientists of unimpeachable international standing were forced to recant their adherence to Mendelian genetics and to conduct their research on the basis of an ideological theory of the environmental determination of species change.[1]

This affair is frequently presented as the epitome of totalitarianism. But the real point is broader: Lysenko's biology would have been no better, and no more legitimate, if it had been imposed by a democratic vote after public deliberation. The political sphere has no rightful authority over the internal processes that guide the quest for truth.

Liberty

In clarifying the scope of democratic political authority, Robert Dahl distinguishes among three different kinds of individual claims to a substantive interest or good. The claim may be to: (1) goods integral to the democratic process, such as freedom of speech or assembly; (2) goods external to the democratic process but necessary for it, such as the possession of the basic resources citizens need to take part in politics; or (3) goods external to the democratic process and not necessary to it.[2]

It is possible to argue that all the individual claims that deserve serious consideration fall into the first two categories.[3] But this view is deeply implausible, and Dahl ultimately rejects it. He acknowledges the existence of important human interests and goods in category 3. And while he is attracted to the view that no interests other than those in categories 1 and 2 should be regarded as binding on democratic publics, he admits that it leaves open a "disturbing question": Can we really assert that human beings "have no inviolable interests beyond their right to the democratic process and whatever is essential to it?"[4]

---

1 For the definitive treatment of this matter, see David Joravsky, *The Lysenko Affair* (Cambridge, Mass.: Harvard University Press, 1970).

2 Dahl, *Democracy and Its Critics* (New Haven, Conn.: Yale University Press, 1989), p. 167.

3 Jurgen Habermas is an example of this mode of thinking. For a discussion and critique of his view that all valid public claims are inherent in the nature of or conditions for democratic deliberation, see Amy Gutmann and Dennis Thompson, *Democracy and Disagreement* (Cambridge, Mass.: Harvard University Press, 1996), pp. 17–18.

4 Dahl, *Democracy and Its Critics*, pp. 182–183.

As an example of what he finds troubling, Dahl offers the example of the right to a fair trial. In Chapter 3 I offered another: a procedurally scrupulous democratic public deliberation on the question of which faith should be adopted as the official state religion. If we are troubled by this prospect, as I think we should be, it is because of our sense that the political order is overriding a fundamental human interest that in nearly all circumstances should remain outside the ambit of political power.[5] To summarize, there are some individual interests that are (a) fundamental human goods, (b) neither intrinsic to nor necessary for democracy, and (c) not evidently subject to democratic authority. These liberties form a second category of activities that challenge and limit the moral scope of democracy.

ALTERNATIVES TO DEMOCRACY WITHIN THE POLITICAL SPHERE

My thesis in this section is that inspection of our actual practices reveals forms of nondemocratic governance that we have good reasons to believe are justified.

Juries

For many purposes, juries are required to reach unanimous judgments. This means that the vote of a single dissenting juror can nullify the votes of eleven others – a weighting system that is hard to square with democracy as ordinarily understood.

It could be otherwise. Socrates was tried before a democratic assembly-jury of 501 and (if the Socratic speech presented by Plato is taken at face value) was convicted by a vote of 280 to 221. Each vote counted equally, and a simple majority sufficed to reach a judgment.

Everyone understands why the nondemocratic U.S. jury system exists, however. Life, liberty, property – these and others are fundamental

---

5 I say "nearly all" because it is possible to imagine (indeed, history records) circumstances in which a community is faced with the choice between mass religious conversion and total annihilation. If I found myself in such circumstances, I would certainly argue that the governing institutions should take up this question on an urgent basis, and I would not argue that it would be a moral breach to establish a state religion. (But not mandatory either; the people would be within their moral rights to choose death over the coerced violation of conscience.)

interests that government exists to protect. A justice system that makes it easy for the state to jeopardize these interests would threaten public purposes that possess a moral standing independent of democratic processes. The U.S. jury system crystallizes this pluralistic moral understanding.

Expertise

There are some public purposes whose effective pursuit requires specialized knowledge and competence that are not widely shared. When the exercise of such expertise is likely to go against the grain of democratic decision making, there may be a case for insulating the experts against the vagaries of democracy. Lifetime tenure for judges is one instance of this; the autonomy of the U.S. Federal Reserve Board is another.

To be sure, the element of democratic accountability is not entirely lacking in either case. And both these institutions are contestable from a democratic point of view. My point is only that good reasons can be adduced in their favor and that these reasons are not straightforwardly democratic. That democratic decision makers can recognize the claims of expertise does not necessarily mean that these claims rest on a democratic foundation – or that the claims would not exist if they were not democratically recognized.

Paternalism

Democracy is thought to give great weight to every citizen's understanding of his or her own interests. From this standpoint, statements of the form "I/we understand your interests better than you do" are inherently suspect.

Nonetheless, U.S. democratic processes have frequently given standing to paternalistic claims. Amy Gutmann and Dennis Thompson offer a nonexhaustive but representative list:

safety laws and regulations (mandating seat belts, ignition interlocks, and air bags, or requiring motorcyclists to wear helmets); health regulations (requiring prescriptions for drugs, and banning certain drugs such as laetrile); criminal law (criminalizing suicide, and disallowing consent as a murder defense); and general social policy (restrictions on gambling, prevention of high-risk recreational activities such as swimming in a local quarry, and licensing of professionals).[6]

To be sure, many of these laws and regulations are controversial. But for the purposes of this argument, I will assume that at least some of them are justifiable, all things considered. My point is that the grounds of their justification are distinct from the bare fact of their democratic authorization. If so, actions consistent with these justificatory reasons may be warranted, even in the absence of democratic authorization.

Consider the following case. While walking through a forest, you come upon two men, one kneeling in a submissive posture, the other pointing a gun at the kneeling man's head and tightening his finger on the trigger. As you rush forward to prevent a tragedy, the kneeling man cries out, "Leave us alone. I gave him permission to shoot me, and you have no right to interfere." I want to suggest that you do have that right, even if no democratically enacted law endorses it. Indeed, I want to go farther: You have the right to interfere, even if a democratic law says that you do not.[7] From a pluralist perspective, there are situations (some paternalist, others not) in which the misguided substance of a democratic decision can trump its legitimating form.

The Common Good

Early in 1861, shortly after the beginning of the Civil War, a mob in Baltimore, Maryland, blocked the movement of troops from Massachusetts heading south to reinforce the defenses of Washington, D.C. At the same time, President Lincoln received credible information that Maryland was moving toward secession. He asked his attorney general for a legal opinion concerning his power to impose martial law or suspend various constitutional rights.

The results were not particularly encouraging. The Constitution did provide (Article I, Section 9) for the suspension of the writ of habeus corpus "when in cases of rebellion or invasion the public safety may require it." But the leading authority of the day, Joseph Story, interpreted the Constitution as empowering only Congress to so act. Story was

6 Gutmann and Thompson, *Democracy and Disagreement*, p. 262.

7 This is not intended as a parable of Oregon's assisted suicide law, which is distinguishable from the men-in-the-forest case in a number of important respects.

joined in this view by most jurists and judges, as well as by the Supreme Court. Nonetheless, on April 25, 1861, President Lincoln sent General Winfield Scott an order authorizing him to suspend habeus corpus in the event that Maryland moved toward rebellion or secession – the first of several such orders over the next two months.

It was not until July that Lincoln presented a formal defense of his action to a special session of Congress. The terms of that defense bring us to the philosophical point:

The whole of the laws which were required to be faithfully executed, were being resisted, and failing of execution, in nearly one-third of the States. Must they be allowed to finally fail of execution, even had it been perfectly clear, that by the use of the means necessary to their execution, some single law, made in such extreme tenderness of the citizen's liberty, that practically, it relieves more of the guilty, than of the innocent, should, to a very limited extent, be violated? . . . [A]re all the laws, *but one*, to go unexecuted, and the government itself go to pieces, lest that one be violated?[8]

The crux of Lincoln's argument was that his duty to preserve the government he led overrode otherwise binding constitutional and democratic requirements: *Salus populi suprema lex*. While Lincoln informed the Congress of his decision and the reasons for it, he did not ask for their approval. To do so would have been to call into question his right to defend the people's most urgent interests in a moment of supreme danger. Even after the Congress finally passed the Habeus Corpus Act almost two years later, in March of 1863, Lincoln continued to defend his conduct on the basis of political and moral obligation, rather than positive law.[9]

If we believe (as I do) that President Lincoln acted correctly, it follows that there are considerations based on the common good of a political community that can justify the violation of otherwise binding democratic norms. Just as the "good life" depends on "mere life," so too does a good ordering of the political community depend on the physical existence and integrity of that community.

This limited legitimation of parademocratic leadership is fraught with risk because it opens the door to the abuse of discretion in the direction

8 Quoted in Mark E. Neely, Jr., *The Fate of Liberty: Abraham Lincoln and Civil Liberties* (New York: Oxford University Press, 1991), p. 12.
9 Ibid., p. 68.

of tyranny. But it is even more dangerous to rule it out altogether. A democratic polity is not a suicide pact.

PLURALIST CONSTITUTIONAL DEMOCRACY

The arguments I have sketched thus far are more suggestive than dispositive. I hope they have at least made a plausible case that there is something important to be learned about the limits of democracy by viewing it through the lens of value pluralism. I turn now to a brief discussion of constitutional democracy itself within the pluralist frame.

Pluralist Constitutionalism

From a pluralist perspective, a democratic constitution represents a decision by the people to elevate a subset of worthy ends, purposes, and values above others, at least for the conduct of public life. For example, the Preamble to the U.S. Constitution focuses on certain core purposes rather than others: "domestic tranquility" but not "fraternity." The governing institutions established by the Constitution rest on a distinctive balance between the desire for effectiveness and the fear of tyrannical power. The Bill of Rights gives special emphasis to specific liberties, especially those involving the administration of justice. And so forth.

Like every constitution, the U.S. Constitution is characterized by an internal pluralism, that is, by a multiplicity of goods none of which is overriding in all circumstances. Consider the portion of the Constitution most often viewed as dominant or absolute – the rights enshrined in the First Amendment. As Laurence Tribe makes clear, it proves impossible in practice to evade the task of weighing those rights against competing public interests. For example, the courts have felt compelled to distinguish among more and less protected categories of speech. But, as Tribe argues, "Any exclusion of a class of activities from first amendment safeguards represents an implicit conclusion that the governmental interests in regulating these activities are such as to justify whatever limitation is thereby placed on the free expression of ideas."[10] Constitutional

---

10 Laurence Tribe, *American Constitutional Law, Second Edition* (Mineola, N.Y.: Foundation Press, 1988), p. 792.

adjudication, then, cannot avoid the essentially deliberative task of weighing and comparing competing values without the guidance of bright lines and lexical priorities.

This does not mean that pluralist constitutionalism is reduced to pure intuitionism. Typically, a line of cases will establish, in general terms, the kind of test constitutional value A must pass to be regarded as weightier than constitutional value B. Courts are exposed to criticism when a particular test violates a widely shared sense of the relative importance of key values. In 1990, for example, the Supreme Court handed down a decision that lowered the burden of proof that government had to discharge in order to enact laws that have the effect of restricting the free exercise of religion. This decision triggered a public furor that led three years later to the enactment of a new statute that, in effect, restored the more stringent prior burden on government efforts to impede religious free exercise.[11]

This depiction of pluralist constitutional adjudication leads to a broader point about deliberation within a pluralist frame. It is not necessary (and probably not possible) to begin deliberation with a promiscuous heap of goods to be rank-ordered on a case-by-case basis. There is an important role for the rough-and-ready guidance provided by the rules of ordinary morality. But these rules must be understood (to put the matter in legal terms) as rebuttable presumptions, rather than inviolable imperatives of action. Pluralist deliberation must be open to the possibility that even the most deeply entrenched principles of conduct may have to be revised or set aside in unusual circumstances. The nature of the reasons that could warrant deviations from normal practices can only be determined with reference to the complex of facts that defines a specific choice situation.

Pluralism and Democratic Deliberation

In the *Nicomachean Ethics,* Aristotle characterizes the proper sphere of deliberation as an arena of uncertainty and unpredictability. We think through a geometry problem, but we do not deliberate about it; we investigate astronomical phenomena, but we do not deliberate about

11 This statute was subsequently ruled unconstitutional by the Supreme Court, and the struggle continues.

them. Nor do we deliberate about whether a pot of water will boil when placed over a hot flame.[12]

If Martha Nussbaum is correct, Aristotelian deliberation extends to the specification of ends as well as the choice of means.[13] That is certainly true for deliberation conducted within the value-pluralist frame. A situation requiring choice will typically present a multiplicity of genuine but heterogeneous human goods, not all of which can be attained (or maximized) simultaneously. Citizens will typically differ among themselves in the rank-order or weight to be attached to these goods. But if they are deliberating reasonably, they will at least agree that the goods in question are all ends worthy of pursuit.

Sometimes deliberative agreement can go farther. I suspect we have all had the experience of sitting in a meeting where some matter requiring choice is being debated. Finally someone speaks so cogently that the debate ends; the speaker has somehow enabled us to see the situation in a way such that a particular course of action emerges as clearly preferable, all things considered.

The deliberative considerations deployed by successful speakers will themselves vary with circumstances. It may be argued that B is more urgent than A, or more important, or less risky; or that an increment of A can be obtained only at excessive cost to B. Value pluralism does not rule out the possibility of right answers in specific situations. But these particularized judgments need not flow from, or lead to, general rules of action.[14]

In many circumstances, however, closure cannot be achieved. Where does that leave democratic deliberation? First, it offers a basis for mutual acceptance. While I may believe that a particular choice among, or weighting of, competing goods is best, I understand that it is not unreasonable for others to arrive at different judgments concerning these goods. Disagreement need not degenerate into imputations of error or fault. Those with whom I disagree are not ignorant, or excessively self-regarding, or shortsighted, or blinded by passion; they just happen to see things differently, as I might have under other circumstances.

12 *Nicomachean Ethics* III. iii. 3–10.
13 Nussbaum, *The Fragility of Goodness: Luck and Ethics in Greek Tragedy and Philosophy* (Cambridge: Cambridge University Press, 1986), pp. 296–297.
14 For this and related matters, see Brian Barry, "*Political Argument* After Twenty-Five Years," in *Political Argument: A Reissue with a New Introduction* (Berkeley: University of California Press, 1990), pp. xxxix–xliv, lxix–lxxii.

Second, to the extent that all parties recognize the values at stake as genuine goods, each will have reasons to be cautious about proposed courses of action that, in effect, assign a weight of zero to one or more of these values. Consider the following example: A small town in the Pacific Northwest is divided between 600 committed environmentalists and 400 third-generation loggers. From a purely majoritarian point of view, it would be possible for the environmentalists to impose strict regulations that would throw all the loggers out of work. But if they accept the fact that the logging jobs are part of a way of life that can reasonably be regarded as desirable (its impact on the environment notwithstanding), they will doubt that it is reasonable to press their majoritarian advantage to the hilt and will look for an alternative course of action that does less violence to the most cherished values of the minority. While value pluralism may not entail a politics of inclusion, it certainly offers a plausible basis for such a politics.

Another consideration points in the same direction. To believe that it is not manifestly unreasonable for others to see the world differently is to acknowledge that one's own views, while perhaps firmly held, fall short of mathematical certainty. That is, there is some chance that the majority that sees things my way may be to some extent mistaken. If so, it is reasonable for the majority to hedge its bets by incorporating some of the minority's views.

Consider an analogy. Suppose there are two cancer researchers pursuing conflicting lines of research: If A's hypothesis is vindicated, B's must be rejected, and vice versa. Even if the National Science Foundation believes that A is considerably more likely to be correct than B, it is reasonable for the NSF to make an investment greater than zero in B's research.[15]

CONCLUSION

In this chapter, I have suggested that three broad political conclusions flow from the acceptance of value pluralism: first, that the legitimate

15 This example was suggested by a discussion in Joseph H. Carens, "Compromises in Politics," in J. Roland Pennock and John W. Chapman, eds., *NOMOS XXI: Compromise in Ethics, Law, and Politics* (New York: New York University Press, 1979). For more systematic reflections on the implications of pluralism for negotiation and compromise, see Richard Bellamy, *Liberalism and Pluralism: Towards a Politics of Compromise* (London: Routledge, 1999).

scope of all politics, democratic politics included, is limited; second, that within the political sphere there are alternatives to democracy that enjoy legitimacy, at least for some purposes in some situations; and third, that democratic deliberation and decision should be guided by mutual acceptance and the quest for inclusive, rather than exclusive, policies.

To be sure, there is a loose-jointedness in the political inferences I draw from value pluralism. I have offered a series of conjectures and analogies that are consistent with pluralism, but in most (perhaps all) cases not entailed by it.

There is one assertion about which I remain steadfast – the propriety of rejoining value theory and political theory. I make no claims as to the priority of either over the other. My point is only that each has a bearing on the other, and that we must strive for consistency between them.

8

PARENTS, GOVERNMENT, AND CHILDREN

Authority over Education in the Liberal Pluralist State

INTRODUCTION

Contemporary debates about education in the United States occur within a context of assumptions that we take for granted without much thought, as follows: The government has the right (and perhaps duty) to require the education of all children up through the midteens and to regulate some basic features of their education. Parents bear principal responsibility for seeing to it that their children meet this requirement, but they have the right to choose among a wide range of options for meeting it. While government has the right to tax all its citizens to finance and operate a system of public schools open to all, it cannot create a public school monopoly that prevents parents from sending their children to nonpublic schools.

Each of these assumptions was contested earlier in our history; all now enjoy near-universal support. In my judgment, this shift represents more than bare historical contingency or practical necessity. These widely accepted assumptions are consistent with liberal pluralist theory, as well as with the practical requirements of life in liberal democracies under modern circumstances.

The underlying theory goes something like this: In establishing the aims of – and control over – education, three sets of considerations must somehow be coordinated. First, the conditions for the normal development of children must be secured, their ability to become contributing members of the economy and society must be fostered, and the growth over time of their capacity for sound independent judgment must be recognized. Second, the liberal democratic state must act not only to safeguard the developmental interests of children but also to promote the effective functioning of its basic institutions. Third, the special relationship between parents and children must be reflected in the allocation of educational authority, and so must what I shall call the "expressive interest" of parents in raising their children in a manner consistent with their understanding of what gives meaning and value to life.

While each of the values must find appropriate expression in practical decisions, there is no guarantee that they will fit together into a harmonious whole. Pressed to the hilt, any one of them will entail costs to the others that may well be judged excessive. Sound education policy cannot be exclusively state-centered, parent-centered, or child-centered. Among other implications, this schema means that civic concerns do not function as trumps in discussions of educational policy. A particular course of action designed to promote important civic objectives may nonetheless be the wrong thing to do for other reasons: For example, the government cannot rightly compel schoolchildren to join in a flag salute ceremony contrary to the dictates of their conscience.[1] This remains the case even if the flag salute proves to be an effective means of fostering patriotism. It is equally true that parental concerns do not function as trumps; in some cases, the damage to core civic concerns, or to the child's interests, will be too extensive. Let me underscore three features of this thesis.

1. Liberal democracies are not civic republics. The liberal democratic state does not have plenipotentiary power, and public-spirited aims need not govern the actions of its citizens in all spheres and circumstances. And while feminism has reinterpreted and relocated the boundary between public and private matters, it does not necessarily deny the appropriateness of the distinction as such or the value of privacy, rightly understood, in human life.[2] If the liberal democratic state were to legislate a conception of child or governmental interests that in effect nullified parental educational choice, it would exceed the legitimate bounds of its authority.

Much the same can be said of liberal democratic justice. Whichever conception of liberal democratic justice one prefers, it cannot be so comprehensive and stringent as to expunge a substantial zone of diversity and choice. Justice establishes a framework of claims that individuals

1 As the Supreme Court recognized in *West Virginia v. Barnette*, 319 U.S. 624 (1943).
2 See Susan Moller Okin, *Justice, Gender, and the Family* (New York: Basic Books, 1989), pp. 127–128.

and (for some purposes) groups may ask the state to enforce. But potential claimants need not press their justified claims to the hilt. They may choose not to exercise some of their entitlements, in return for other goods that seem preferable, all things considered. The proposition "It would be unjust for you to deprive me of A" does not imply the conclusion "It would be wrong for me not to exercise my claim to A against you." The nonexercise of a justified claim becomes questionable only when the potential claimant is subject to intimidation or is deprived of the information and self-confidence required for independent judgment. The free exercise of independent and group choice within the framework of liberal democratic judgment generates a zone of diverse ways of life that are permissible and safeguarded from external intervention, even when we could not imagine choosing them for ourselves. Liberal democracy as I understand it is particularly sensitive to this moral diversity and to the importance of social spaces within which it may find expression. If so, I might add, liberal democratic civic education must emphasize the beliefs and virtues that enable citizens to respect the boundaries of free social spaces.

2. When I invoke parental authority over education, I presuppose a fair division of decision-making power between the parents (assuming that more than one is in the picture). I make no assumptions about who can be a parent, about how one becomes a parent, or about the parent's legal status in relation to another parent or to the child. I do not address the circumstances in which the presumption in favor of the parent may be rebutted by parental misconduct or incapacity. Nor do I intend to enter into, or to prejudge, the knotty questions that arise when marriages dissolve or when a child's relatives other than parents (grandparents, for example) make claims on a share of decision-making authority. My discussion, then, takes place within a simplified model of family life. I leave for another occasion the question of how my arguments and conclusions would change in response to various real-world alterations of the model.

3. To insist, as I do, that control over education is a function of distinct and sometimes competing normative dimensions is to say almost nothing about how these variables should be weighted or rank-ordered in determining individual decisions. This gap can be filled only by thick descriptions of specific decision contexts and by deliberative arguments about the relative importance of different dimensions of value within

these contexts. Even after careful description and deliberation, in many situations it will not prove possible to reach full closure, leaving wide latitude for appropriate processes of political decision making.

While the multivalued pluralist perspective I am urging is not enough to produce unique affirmative results, it does yield an important negative consequence. This approach makes it impossible to argue directly from the premise "Option A yields important gains along dimension X" to the conclusion "We should choose A," because others may reasonably contend that the sacrifices of value along other dimensions are significant enough to outweigh the gains along X. From this perspective, then, it never suffices to claim that a particular course of action serves the interests of children, or parents, or civic life; all must somehow be taken into account.

EDUCATION IN U.S. HISTORY

John Stuart Mill regarded the right of the state to compel parents to educate their children as "almost a self-evident axiom." Yet writing in 1859, he observed that in practice, few of his fellows citizens were willing to affirm its force. While most acknowledged the moral duty of parents to educate their children, they denied that the state had the right to enforce it.[3] Much the same situation prevailed on the other side of the Atlantic. Despite the spread of the "common school" ideal in the early decades of the nineteenth century, by as late as the eve of the Civil War only two states (Massachusetts and New York) had enacted compulsory education statutes.[4] Many citizens who conceded that this policy would promote the general welfare nonetheless denied that the state could properly – and constitutionally – go down this road.

Within decades, matters had changed radically. By 1900, thirty-two states had passed compulsory attendance laws. By 1918, such laws were universal throughout the United States. Despite its readiness to strike down a wide range of social legislation as infringements of individual liberty, not even the Lochner-era Supreme Court was willing to raise constitutional questions about the power of the states to enforce such

3 John Stuart Mill, *On Liberty*, ed. Currin V. Shields (Indianapolis: Bobbs-Merrill, 1956), p. 128.
4 R. Freeman Butts and Lawrence A. Cremin, *A History of Education in American Culture* (New York: Holt, Rinehart and Winston, 1953), p. 415.

laws. Given the late development of the policy of universal compulsory education, this agreement is all the more noteworthy.

It is instructive to review the kinds of arguments in favor of public education that gained currency in the century between the onset of the common school debate and the establishment of universal compulsory education. The first may be called "limited perfectionism": A certain measure of education was necessary for normal intellectual and moral development and for full participation in cultural and associational life. The second revolved around basic social obligations: Education enabled individuals to maintain their economic independence and to discharge their duties to family members. Third, education was thought to promote a range of public goods: economic growth, appropriate civic beliefs and virtues, national unity and "Americanization," and a strong national defense. The increased credibility of these claims represented a response to key developments – in particular, the industrialization of the economy, the diversification of the population through immigration, and the emergence of the United States in world affairs.

FROM HISTORY TO THEORY

Mill regards it as virtually self-evident that the state "should require and compel the education, up to a certain standard, of every human being who is born its citizen." In his account, the state's authority derives from parental responsibility. The bare fact of causing the existence of another human being brings into play more responsibilities than does virtually any other human act.[5] In particular, "it is one of the most sacred duties of the parents (or, as law and usage now stand, the father), after summoning a human being into the world, to give to that being an education fitting him to perform his part well in life toward others and toward himself." The failure to do so is a "moral crime, both against the unfortunate offspring and against society; and . . . if the parent does not fulfill this obligation, the State ought to see it fulfilled."[6]

Mill assumes that this educational duty flows directly from the fact of biological generation, coupled with broad features of the individual and social good. Parents do not have the right to neglect the education of their children in ways that impose avoidable burdens on their

5 Mill, *On Liberty*, p. 128.
6 Ibid.

fellow citizens – for example, by raising children unable to contribute to the economy or unwilling to obey the law. Nor do they have the right to deprive their children of what Mill assumes to be the profound and pervasive benefits of education: The development of human faculties is at the core of what he terms the "permanent interests of man as a progressive being."[7] Mill accepts a version of the thesis I earlier termed limited perfectionism; the necessity of education reflects not only the contextually specific requisites of advanced economies but also noncontextual features of the human condition. The state has a legitimate interest in enforcing parental responsibility, both to enhance social utility and to create human beings in the "maturity of their faculties" who are "capable of being improved by free and equal discussion."[8]

Mill suggests that this parental responsibility is material as well as moral: Parents must finance their children's education to the extent they can. His insistence on individual responsibility is striking: The "moral crime" lies not only in willfully depriving a child of education but also in bringing a child into the world without a "fair prospect" of being able to afford a basic education. (He even endorses the legitimacy of European laws forbidding couples to marry unless they have the means to support a family.)[9] But he also stresses the element of social responsibility: When the state makes education compulsory, it must provide sliding-scale subsidies for lower-income families and pay outright for the education of children whose parents cannot afford to contribute anything. So all members of the society must do their part to sustain a system of compulsory education that benefits society as a whole.

Mill distinguishes between state-enforced compulsory education and direct state provision of education. He opposes all policies that lead to state dominance over or monopoly of education. Diversity of character and opinion is the key to both individual flourishing and social progress. But a state-dominated system of education is a "mere contrivance for molding people to be exactly like one another" that "establishes a despotism over the mind." A state system of education "should only exist, if it exist at all, as one among many competing experiments, carried on for

7 Ibid., p. 14.
8 Ibid., pp. 13, 14.
9 Ibid., p. 132.

the purpose of example and stimulus to keep the others up to a certain standard of excellence."[10]

This is not to say that the state has no interest in defining a basic common education or no legitimate power to enforce it. A wide range of parental choice makes sense only in the context of public-defined educational standards that can serve as regular and reliable benchmarks of educational attainment. Mill proposes a universal system of public examinations, beginning with basic literacy at an early age and widening out annually to ensure the acquisition and retention of core general knowledge. He is confident that these examinations can be structured to prevent the state from exercising an improper, homogenizing control over the formation of opinion, through a strict focus on "positive science." To the extent that examinations on such disputed topics as religion and politics are administered, for example, they should be confined to facts about the views of specific authors or denominations and the stated grounds of those views.[11]

Clearly, Mill is offering a generalized defense of educational diversity and parental choice. But what kind of theory is it? At first glance, Mill's theory is child-centered: A state educational monopoly disserves the best interests of children because it is bound to foster mental despotism and personal unhappiness by repressing individuality. By implication, Mill's account of individuality rejects the thesis that individual identity is socially constructed. Rather, each of us is born with a "nature" – a distinctive ensemble of talents, dispositions, and potentialities of character. To the extent that this ensemble is able to flourish, our lives gain value, for ourselves and for those around us. If not, our capacities wither and starve, and we lose touch with ourselves.

One may, of course, question Mill's point of departure. But there is much to be said in favor of the proposition that children are not uniform blank slates that others may inscribe as they please. Most parents are led by their own experience to acknowledge the existence and importance of each child's distinctive natural bent. Good parenting – and by extension good education – finds ways of accomplishing its essential purposes with, rather than against, the grain.

10 Ibid., p. 129.
11 Ibid., pp. 130–131.

The crucial issue is whether our upbringing will accommodate and encourage or, rather, pinch and repress the development of our distinctiveness. But there is no guarantee that a system of parental educational choice would promote individuality as Mill understands it. He is critical of patriarchy, but he does not draw the obvious connection that a father's choice may prove just as procrustean for a child as would the state's. Instead of a single despotic power there might be a multiplicity of smaller ones. (Mill of all people should have been exquisitely sensitive to this possibility.) Mill's proposed system would promote educational diversity, to be sure, but not necessarily individuality.

There is more to be said in defense of Mill's position, however. Educational diversity is at least a necessary condition for the cultivation of individuality. Assuming, as Mill does, the diversity of human types, it is hard to see how any single unitary system of education could accommodate all of them equally well. The existence of a range of educational choices offers the possibility of a better fit between institutional settings and individual needs.

Although children can be consulted, moreover, they cannot make these choices for themselves, especially in the early years. Either parents will make these choices or the state will choose for them. While parents may often fail to choose wisely, there are reasons to believe that the state typically will do even worse. On average, parents understand their children's individual traits better than public authorities do, their concern for their children's well-being is deeper, and they are not subject to the homogenizing imperatives of even the best bureaucracies in the modern state. In practice, the legal system must create a presumption in one direction or the other, and the case for a presumption in favor of parents is strong.

But rebuttable. While the range of parental discretion is wide, the state properly enforces numerous limits on parental authority. Laws against abuse and neglect mean that parents are not free to injure their children or to deprive them of the basic goods needed for normal physical, mental, and emotional development. Nor may parents invoke their deepest religious convictions to prevent their children's immunization or deprive them of essential medical care. By the same token, the state may act to prevent what amounts to educational abuse and neglect, by means of such measures as compulsory education statutes and basic standards of education attainment. But the state cannot legitimately define a concept of the child's best interests so extensive and detailed that its enforcement would, in practice, eviscerate the power of parents to make decisions concerning their children's education.

Eamonn Callan offers a useful example: Suppose that the parents of a musically talented child can afford either to buy a piano or to take her on an expensive holiday. Judged from the standpoint of the developmental best interests of the child, the right choice is reasonably clear. But we draw the line at state authority with the power to compel parents to buy the piano instead of going to Disneyland. There must, it appears, be a protected zone of parental discretion, even when the judgments parents make look mistaken to outsiders.[12]

Why should such a zone exist? One standard liberal answer is fear of the overweening state: Even if the judgment of bureaucratic experts were systematically superior to that of parents, a government with the power to make us buy the piano is unlikely to leave any of our liberties intact. But a fuller answer includes as well the interests of parents in raising children in a manner consistent with their own understanding. It is to this theme that I now turn.

EXPRESSIVE LIBERTY AND PARENTAL INTERESTS

In Chapter 3 I defined the value category of "expressive liberty." Let me restate the essentials of that account.

By expressive liberty I mean the absence of constraints imposed by some individuals or groups on others that make it impossible or significantly more difficult for the affected individuals or groups to live their lives in ways that express their deepest beliefs about what gives meaning and value to life. Expressive liberty offers us the opportunity to enjoy a fit between inner and outer, conviction and deed. Not all sets of practices will themselves rest on, or reflect a preference for, liberty as ordinarily understood. Expressive liberty protects the ability of individuals and groups to live in ways that others would regard as unfree.

Expressive liberty is an important value because it is a precondition for leading a complete and satisfying life. The reason is straightforward: Part of what it means to have deep beliefs about how one should live is the desire to live in accordance with them.

12 Eamonn Callan, *Creating Citizens: Political Education and Liberal Democracy* (Oxford: Clarendon Press, 1997), pp. 146–147.

Although expressive liberty is a great good, it is not the only good, and it is certainly not without limits. No one would seriously argue that the expressive liberty of parents would legitimate the ritual sacrifice of their children or that expressive liberty can be invoked to blunt the force of responsibility to our fellow citizens and to legitimate public institutions. But because it is a core value, it cannot rightly be infringed absent countervailing reasons of considerable weight.

Expressive liberty is possible only within societies whose members do not needlessly impede one another's opportunity to live their lives as they see fit. Citizens must internalize norms – not of substantive indifference, but rather of self-restraint – in the face of practices that reflect understandings of the good life that they reject. Fostering this self-restraint – the principled refusal to use individual or collective coercion to deprive others of expressive liberty – is a legitimate object of liberal civic action.

What I want to argue is that the ability of parents to raise their children in a manner consistent with their deepest commitments is an essential element of expressive liberty. As Eamonn Callan rightly suggests, parenting is typically undertaken as one of the central meaning-giving tasks of our lives. We cannot detach our aspirations for our children from our understanding of what is good and virtuous. As Stephen Gilles insists, loving and nurturing a child cannot in practice be divorced from shaping that child's values. In so doing as parents, we cannot but draw on the comprehensive understanding that gives our values whatever coherence and grounding they may possess.[13] Moreover, we hope for relations of intimacy with our children, as they develop and when they are grown. But estrangement is the enemy of intimacy. It is understandable for parents to fear that their children may become embroiled in ways of life they regard as alien and distasteful and, within limits, to act to reduce the risk that this fear will be realized. Callan links these parental expressive interests with core liberal freedoms:

The rights to freedom of conscience and association are widely accepted as among the necessary requirements of any recognizably liberal regime. But the freedom to rear our children according to the dictates of conscience is for most of us as important as any other expression of conscience, and the freedom to organize and sustain the life of the family in keeping with our own values is

13 Stephen G. Gilles, "On Educating Children: A Parentalist Manifesto," *University of Chicago Law Review* 63 (1996): 960–961.

as significant as our liberty to associate outside the family for any purpose whatever.[14]

Conversely, one of the most disturbing features of illiberal regimes is the wedge their governments typically seek to drive between parents and children, and the effort they make to replace a multiplicity of family traditions with a unitary, state-administered culture.

The appropriate parental role is structured in part by the vulnerability, dependency, and developmental needs of children. The model of fiduciary responsibility developed by Locke and endorsed by such contemporary thinkers as Richard Arneson and Ian Shapiro well captures this dimension of the parent–child relationship.[15] But the expressive interests of parents are not reducible to their fiduciary duty to promote their children's interests. A better model is more nearly reciprocal: Parents and children serve, and are served by, one another in complex ways. To quote Callan once more:

[I]f a moral theory interprets the child's role so as to make individual children no more than instruments of their parents' good it would be open to damning moral objections. But parallel objections must be decisive against any theory that interprets the parent's role in ways that make individual parents no more than instruments of their children's good. We should want a conception of parents' rights in education that will not license the oppression of children. But we should also want a conception that will do justice to the hopes that parents have and the sacrifices they make in rearing their children.[16]

This reciprocity model must do justice to the particularity of the relationship between specific parents and specific children. Everyone can agree that children are not the "property" of their parents. Still, when I say that this child is "mine," I am both acknowledging responsibilities and asserting authority beyond what I owe or claim vis-à-vis children in general. As parent, I am more than the child's caretaker or teacher, and I am not simply a representative of the state delegated to prepare the child for citizenship. The hopes and sacrifices to which Callan refers reflect the intimate particularity of the parent–child bond, the fact that the child is in part (though only in part) an extension of ourselves.

---

14 Callan, *Creating Citizens,* p. 143.
15 See "Democratic Autonomy and Religious Freedom: A Critique of *Wisconsin v. Yoder,*" in Ian Shapiro, *Democracy's Place* (Ithaca, N.Y.: Cornell University Press, 1996), Chapter 6.
16 Callan, *Creating Citizens,* p. 145.

This fact helps explain the multiplicity of moral claims that sons and daughters must balance: to themselves (the duty of integrity), to the state (the responsibilities of citizenship), and to their parents (the obligation of gratitude, if not always obedience).

Like any other value, the expressive interests of parents can be pushed too far. To begin with, as children develop, their own expressive interests must be given increased weight. Consider the well-known case of *Wisconsin v. Yoder*. This case presented a clash between a Wisconsin state law, which required school attendance until age sixteen, and three Old Order Amish parents, who claimed that mandating their children's school attendance after age fourteen would undermine their community-based religious practices. While the Supreme Court decided in favor of the parents, a number of justices declared that the adolescent children had liberty claims independent of their parents. The record offered no evidence of religious disagreement between the Amish children and their parents. If the children had expressed the desire to continue their education, these justices would have voted to uphold the state's enforcement of its attendance laws against the wishes of the parents. At a minimum, the children's freestanding religious claims imply enforceable rights of exit from the boundaries of community defined by their parents. I would add that the exit rights must be more than formal. Communities cannot rightly act in ways that disempower individuals – intellectually, emotionally, or practically – from living successfully outside their bounds.

But should the expressed views of the children be taken as dispositive? Richard Arneson and Ian Shapiro say not: Even if the children acquiesce, the parents may still be in violation of their fiduciary responsibility. A parent, they insist, cannot pretend to speak for the child while really regarding the child as an empty vessel for the parent's own religious convictions. As a fiduciary, the parent is bound to preserve the child's own future religious freedom.[17]

Even if we accept this premise (and it may be questioned from several perspectives), it is by no means clear what practical conclusions we are compelled to draw from it. Does respect for a child's religious freedom mean that the parent is required to treat all comprehensive views equally, taking the child on a tour of different faiths and secular philosophical

17 Arneson and Shapiro, "Democratic Autonomy and Religious Freedom," p. 154.

outlooks and then saying, in effect, you choose? Few parents, whatever their outlook, would accept this proposition; even fewer would endorse its enforcement by the state. And I do not see considerations weighty enough to warrant such a sharp break with established practices. At the very least, parents are entitled to introduce their children to what they regard as vital sources of meaning and value, and to hope that their children will come to share this orientation. One might also argue that instructing children within a particular tradition, far from undermining intellectual or religious freedom, may in fact promote it. Knowing what it means to live within a coherent framework of value and belief may well contribute to an informed adult choice between one's tradition of origin and those encountered later in life.

Now consider a thought experiment at the other extreme. Suppose a group raises its children with the result that as adults, none ever questions or rejects the group's basic orientation. To achieve this result, the group seals itself off from the outside world and structures its internal education so that children are not even aware of alternatives to the group's way of life. In effect, the group has become a kind of mental and moral prison. Because diversity and disagreement typically arise even in circumstances of considerable repression, their absence in this case is a sign of extreme suppression of individuality that warrants external scrutiny and perhaps intervention. Parents abuse their expressive liberty if they turn their children into automatons, in part because in so doing, they deprive their children of the opportunity to exercise their own expressive liberty.

In this respect, I agree with Eamonn Callan's argument that servility is a vice and that parental actions fostering servility in children amount to illegitimate despotism. As a parent, I cannot rightly mold my child's character in a way that effectively preempts "serious thought at any future date about the alternatives to my judgement." Every child has a prospective interest in personal sovereignty (Callan's term) or, in my term, expressive liberty, that parents cannot rightly undermine.[18]

There are, however, formative forces other than parental despotism that also foster servility. Children immersed in a culture defined by advertising, entertainment media, and peer pressure are often dominated by influences that they neither understand nor resist. In the face

18 Callan, *Creating Citizens,* pp. 152–154.

of such challenges, to have any realistic possibility of exerting countervailing formative power, parents may be compelled to take a strong countercultural stance that involves a substantial measures of family or communal separation from external influences. Parental actions that may be judged despotic in some circumstances may well be necessary, or at least justified, in others.

While these arguments clarify some moral intuitions, they also suggest that practical issues of educational authority cannot be resolved on the plane of moral abstractions. The acceptability of parental decisions must be evaluated within the full context of influences shaping children's awareness of alternatives and ability to weight them. And it is not enough to judge the intention of parents' educational decisions; we must also look at their concrete results.

These considerations highlight some relevant empirical dimensions of the *Yoder* controversy. The Amish community is not a prison. Young adults must explicitly choose to become full members. Substantial numbers decide not to join at the threshold, and others leave later. While there are transitional difficulties for some, there is no evidence that many former members find themselves unable to cope with the demands of a modern economy and society.

This is hardly surprising. In a contemporary liberal democratic society, it is impossible for small groups to seal themselves off from ways of life very different from their own. At most, even a coherent separationist community, such as the Amish, can serve as a counterweight to the dominant culture. It cannot prevent children from learning about alternatives, and while it can offer young adults various incentives to stay, it cannot prevent them from leaving.

Even if *Yoder* does not violate the present or potential expressive liberty of Amish young people, it may be argued that the decision gives inadequate weight to the state's interest in fostering good citizens. According to this line of argument, good citizens participate actively in public affairs, using developed powers of critical reason to deliberate on and decide among competing policies and representatives. But Amish education discourages both active participation and critical reasoning and thus fails to meet legitimate basic state requirements.[19]

19 This is the core of Arneson and Shapiro's critique of *Yoder*.

There are three sorts of reply to this line of argument. First, as we have seen, the proposition that X is instrumental to (or even necessary for) the creation of good citizens does not, as a matter of constitutional law or liberal democratic theory, warrant the conclusion that X is right or legitimate, all things considered. There may be compelling moral and human considerations that prevent the state from enforcing otherwise acceptable policies on dissenting individuals or groups.

Second, even if we accept the premise that critical reasoning is a sine qua non of liberal democratic citizenship, there is no reason to believe that the Amish are incapable of exercising it, in the relevant respect. I recently read a newspaper article (regrettably I cannot locate the reference) written by a Catholic theologian concerning U.S. tactics in the Kosovo conflict. Reasoning from and applying the principles of Catholic "justice in war" doctrine, he concluded that high-altitude bombing safeguarded pilots at a morally unacceptable cost in civilian lives. This is an example of critical reasoning *within* or *from* a tradition, rather than *about* that tradition. But it would be unreasonable for a conception – especially an enforceable conception – of liberal democratic citizenship to demand that citizens somehow set aside, or adopt a stance of open-minded neutrality toward, the beliefs around which they organize they lives when reasoning about public affairs. The Amish have demonstrated their capacity for critical reasoning in the ways that it is publicly reasonable to expect it.[20]

And finally, the active deliberative/participatory virtues are not the only virtues of citizenship we should care about. Law-abidingness, personal and family responsibility, and tolerance of social diversity are also important for the successful functioning of contemporary liberal democracies.[21] In these respects, among others, the Amish score high. They may not be the best of citizens, but may we not say that they are good enough? At least they fulfill the political version of the Hippocratic oath – to do no harm. I might add that if nonvoting and civic withdrawal are taken as sufficient evidence of parental and pedagogical failure warranting state intervention, then our indictment extends far beyond the

20 See, for example, the essays assembled in Albert N. Keim, ed., *Compulsory Education and the Amish: The Right Not to Be Modern* (Boston: Beacon Press, 1975).
21 See William A. Galston, *Liberal Purposes: Goods, Virtues, and Diversity in the Liberal State* (Cambridge: Cambridge University Press, 1991), Chapter 10.

minute numbers of Amish to implicate more than half the families and graduates of public schools in the United States.

PARENTAL AUTHORITY, EXPRESSIVE LIBERTY, AND PUBLIC EDUCATION

Today, after two decades of hand-wringing about the quality of public education, roughly 90 percent of all school-age children still attend public schools. There is no compelling reason to believe that the emphasis I have placed on expressive liberty and the role of parents, if taken as the basis for actual policy, would significantly erode the dominant position the public schools now enjoy. Nor does my thesis undermine the legitimate role of the state in requiring all parents to educate their children and in establishing basic standards for all educational institutions. (In these important respects, all elementary and secondary education in the United States is "public.") Rather, my account merely makes explicit the moral and theoretical underpinnings of the long-standing U.S. constitutional commitment to the principle that parents may choose among a range of options – public and private, secular and religious, heterogeneous and homogeneous – for discharging their obligation to educate their children.

Nonetheless, my stance does reflect an underlying understanding that some may find objectionable. I believe that in a society characterized by a deep diversity of moral and religious views, and accordingly by diverse family and communal ways of life, considerations of both practical viability and normative legitimacy require that to the maximum extent consistent with the maintenance of civic unity and stability, all permissible ways of life are able to find expression in the key choices families and communities must make. Among these choices, the venue and conduct of education ranks high. I would argue that genuine civic unity rests on unforced consent. States that permit their citizens to live in ways that express their values are likely to enjoy widespread support, even gratitude. By contrast, state coercion is likely to produce dissent, resistance, and withdrawal.

Granted, sometimes the state has no choice. If families, schools, or local communities are acting in ways that violate the basic rights of citizens, then the state must step in. And if the result is resistance – even "massive resistance" in the face of compulsory school desegregation – that is the price that must be paid for defending the rightful claims of all citizens. My point is, rather, that the state must be parsimonious in defining the realm in which uniformity must be secured through coercion. An educational program based on an expansive and contestable definition of good citizenship or civic unity will not ordinarily justify the forcible suppression of expressive liberty.

9

FREEDOM OF ASSOCIATION AND EXPRESSIVE LIBERTY

THE LIBERAL PLURALIST STATE AND FREEDOM OF ASSOCIATION

A liberal pluralist state will contain numerous associations embodying very different conceptions of the ways in which human beings ought to relate to one another and of the goals they ought to pursue. This raises the issue of the proper relation between the state's general public principles and the particular principles that guide the diverse subcommunities. Before exploring this issue systematically, I want to reflect briefly on the reasons that it seems so pressing in the United States today.

To begin with, the past decade has witnessed an increasing awareness of the existence and importance of civil society – that network of intimate, expressive, and associational institutions that stand between the individual and the state. The indigenous American discussion of this sphere goes back to Tocqueville; interest in it has been reinforced by Catholic social thought, by the events of the past decade in Eastern Europe and the former Soviet Union, and by the felt inadequacies both of contemporary hyperindividualism and of our national public life.

At the same time, three converging trends have turned this sphere into a flash point. U.S. civil society is becoming increasingly diverse; previously marginalized or minority groups are becoming increasingly assertive; and the reach of public authority is expanding into areas that were once considered substantially private. The application of general public principles to diverse associations, never a simple matter, is perhaps more complex now than ever before. The definition of common citizenship and of compelling public purposes is accordingly more urgent.

Within liberal pluralist orders (as in all others), there must be some encompassing political norms. The question is how "thick" the political is to be. The answer will help determine the scope of legitimate state intervention in the lives of individuals, and in the internal processes of organizations that make up civil society.

The constitutional politics of liberal pluralism will seek to restrict enforceable general norms to the essentials. By this standard, the grounds for national political norms and state intervention include basic order and physical protection; the sorts of goods that Hampshire, Hart, and others have identified as necessary for tolerable individual and collective life; and the components of shared national citizenship. It is difficult, after all, to see how societies can endure without some measure of order and material decency. And since Aristotle's classic discussion of the matter, it has been evident that political communities are organized around conceptions of citizenship that they must defend, and also nurture through educational institutions, as well as by less visible formative processes.

But how much farther should the state go in enforcing specific conceptions of justice, authority, or the good life? What kinds of differences should the state permit? What kinds of differences may the state encourage or support? I want to suggest that an understanding of liberal pluralism guided by principles of expressive liberty, moral pluralism, and the political pluralism of divided sovereignty yields clear and challenging answers in specific cases.

Let me begin with a simple example. While we may regret the exclusion of women from the Catholic priesthood and from the rabbinate of Orthodox Judaism, I take it that we would agree that otherwise binding antidiscrimination laws should not be invoked to end these practices. What blocks the extension of these laws is our belief that religious associations (and perhaps others as well) enjoy considerable authority within their own sphere to determine their own affairs and in so doing to express their understanding of spiritual matters. We can believe this without necessarily endorsing the specific interpretation of gender roles and relations embedded in broader religious commitments.[1]

---

1 For an important collection of essays, many generally sympathetic to the accommodationist position, see Nancy L. Rosenblum, ed., *Obligations of Citizenship and Demands of Faith* (Princeton, N.J.: Princeton University Press, 2000). For the most systematic

The U.S. Supreme Court has recognized rights of association that limit the purview of otherwise applicable public principles. For example, in *Roberts v. U.S. Jaycees,* the Court enunciated a notion of "expressive" freedom of association as a category worthy of protection as an important counterweight to potentially overweening state power:

According protection to collective effort on behalf of shared goals is especially important in preserving political and cultural diversity and in shielding dissident expression from suppression by the majority. . . . Consequently, we have long understood as implicit in the right to engage in activities protected by the First Amendment a corresponding right to associate with others in pursuit of a wide variety of political, social, economic, educational, religious, and cultural ends. . . . Freedom of association . . . plainly presupposes a freedom not to associate.[2]

Beyond general rights of free association, there are limits on the polity's ability to enforce even core public commitments on subcommunities when these principles clash with religious convictions. Consider, for example, Bob Jones University, whose students were prohibited on religious grounds from engaging in interracial dating. In many cases of conflict between First Amendment–protected associations and compelling state interests, such as ending racial segregation, the flat prohibition of conduct judged obnoxious by public principles seems hard to square with the minimum requirements of Free Exercise. But associations conducting their internal affairs in a manner contrary to core public purposes can legitimately be burdened, even if not banned outright. In such cases, a policy of what might be called "reverse exemption" – that is, the removal of all forms of otherwise applicable public encouragement and favor – may well be the most appropriate course. As the Supreme Court declared in its decision denying Bob Jones's request for reinstatement of its federal tax exemption, "the Government has a fundamental, overriding interest in eradicating racial discrimination [that]

argument against this position, see Brian Barry, *Culture and Equality: An Egalitarian Critique of Multiculturalism* (Cambridge, Mass.: Harvard University Press, 2001), especially Chapter 2. For a response to Barry, see my review in *The Public Interest* 144 (Summer 2001): 100–108.

2 *Roberts v. U.S. Jaycees,* 468 U.S. (1984), 622–623. For two superb discussions of the issues raised by this case, see the essays by George Kateb and Nancy Rosenblum in Amy Gutmann, ed., *Freedom of Association* (Princeton, N.J.: Princeton University Press, 1998).

substantially outweighs whatever burden denial of tax benefits places on petitioners' exercise of their religious beliefs."[3]

Let's move to a less clear-cut example. Consider the issues raised in the case of *Ohio Civil Rights Commission v. Dayton Christian Schools, Inc.*[4] A private fundamentalist school decided not to renew the contract of a pregnant married teacher because of its religiously based belief that mothers with young children should not work outside their homes. After receiving a complaint from the teacher, the Civil Rights Commission investigated, found probable cause to conclude that the school had discriminated against an employee on the basis of religion, and proposed a consent order including full reinstatement with back pay.

As Frederick Mark Gedicks observes, this case involves a clash between a general public norm (nondiscrimination) and the constitutive beliefs of a civil association. The teacher unquestionably experienced serious injury through loss of employment. On the other hand, forcing the school to rehire her would clearly impair the ability of the religious community of which it formed a key part to exercise its distinctive religious views – not just to profess them but also to express them in its practices. The imposition of state-endorsed beliefs on that community would threaten core functions of diverse civil associations – the expression of a range of conceptions of the good life and the mitigation of state power. In this case and others like it, a liberal pluralist politics and jurisprudence would give priority to the claims of civil associations.[5]

Current U.S. federal legislation and constitutional doctrine reflect this priority to a considerable degree. Thus, although Title VII of the Civil Rights Act prohibits employment discrimination on the basis of religion, section 702 of the statute exempts religious organizations. In the case of *Corporation of the Presiding Bishop v. Amos*,[6] decided in 1987, the Supreme Court not only upheld this accommodation in principle but also extended its reach to a wide range of secular activities conducted under the aegis of religious organizations.[7]

---

3 461 U.S. 574 (1983), at 604.

4 477 U.S. 619 (1986).

5 Frederick Mark Gedicks, "Toward a Constitutional Jurisprudence of Religious Group Rights," *Wisconsin Law Review* 99 (1989): 101–103.

6 483 U.S. 327 (1987).

7 For an argument (from a scholar generally sympathetic to wide associational liberty) that *Amos* goes too far, see Nancy L. Rosenblum, "*Amos*: Religious Autonomy and the Moral

This does not mean that all religiously motivated practices are deserving of accommodation. Some clearly are not. Civil associations cannot be permitted to engage in human sacrifice. Nor can a civil association endanger the basic interests of children by withholding medical treatment in life-threatening situations. But there is a basic distinction between the minimal content of the human good, which the state must defend, and diverse conceptions of flourishing above that baseline, which the state must accommodate to the maximum extent possible. There is room for reasonable disagreement as to where that line should be drawn. But an account of liberalism built on expressive liberty and on moral and political pluralism should make us very cautious about expanding the scope of state power in ways that mandate uniformity.

The expansion of the modern state means that most civil associations are now entangled with it in one way or another. If limited (even involuntary) participation in public programs requires civil associations to govern the totality of their internal affairs in accordance with general public principles, then the zone of legitimate diversity is dangerously narrowed. A liberal pluralist jurisprudence consistent with the overall theory I am defending would limit the reach of public principles to those areas in which (for example) civil associations are participating directly and substantially in programs that confer public benefits on their members.

EXPRESSIVE LIBERTY AND CIVIC UNITY IN THE LIBERAL PLURALIST STATE

Let me now turn to one of the most discussed recent examples of the tension between the expressive and civic dimensions of liberal democracy – the controversy between Christian fundamentalist parents and the public schools that erupted in Hawkins County, Tennessee, a decade ago. The parents charged that textbooks selected by the school board conveyed teachings at odds with the faith they sought to transmit to their children. They requested that their children be allowed to use alternative textbooks and (if necessary) study the contested subjects outside the regular classroom. After early efforts by individual school administrators to accommodate the parents' request had collapsed, a legal process

Uses of Pluralism," in Rosenblum, ed., *Obligations of Citizenship and Demands of Faith*, Chapter 6.

ensued that culminated in a pro–school board decision by the U.S. Sixth Circuit Court of Appeals.

The most systematic philosophical analysis of this controversy is offered by Amy Gutmann and Dennis Thompson in the course of their path-breaking account of deliberative democracy. Gutmann and Thompson contend that fidelity to democratic deliberation, as they define it, entails the rejection of the fundamentalists' attempts to have their children shielded from reading materials they found offensive to their faith. The question I want to raise is whether their conception of democratic deliberation proves in the end to be compatible with an understanding of liberalism based on expressive liberty and moral and political pluralism. I conclude that it is not and offer in its place a more capacious account of liberal democratic public argument.

The linchpin of Gutmann and Thompson's account of deliberation is the idea of reciprocity. Building on the work of Rawls and Scanlon, they say that the

foundation of reciprocity is the capacity to seek fair terms of social cooperation for their own sake.... From a deliberative perspective, a citizen offers reasons that can be accepted by others who are similarly motivated to find reasons that can be accepted by others.... [Thus,] a deliberative perspective does not address people who reject the aim of finding fair terms for social cooperation; it cannot reach those who refuse to press their public claims in terms accessible to their fellow citizens.[8]

This understanding of reciprocity raises some deep questions (for example, about the nature of moral motivation), but I won't pursue them here. Instead, staying within the bounds of Gutmann and Thompson's account, I want to offer three caveats. First, the phrase "social cooperation" tends to suggest a common course of action that all citizens (must) pursue. But there are other equally legitimate forms of cooperation, including agreements to disagree, to go our various ways without hindrance or cavil, to "live and let live."

In addition, there are different kinds of "public claims." Individuals may argue that the political community as a whole ought to pursue a particular course of action. (This is, I think, the core case that Gutmann and Thompson have in mind.) But they may also argue that the question

8 Amy Gutmann and Dennis Thompson, *Democracy and Disagreement* (Cambridge, Mass.: Harvard University Press, 1996), pp. 52–53, 55.

at hand should not be treated as a public matter in the first place; or that even if it is a legitimate public matter, some individuals and groups may (or must) be exempted from the constraints of otherwise general decisions. Some public claims are "offensive" – you (all) should do what I say – while others are "defensive" – I need not do what you say, even if you speak in the voice of the entire political community. The kinds of reasons offered in support of defensive claims may rightly differ from those for offensive claims.

Finally, the requirement that the terms of public argument should be "accessible" to one's fellow citizens turns out to be highly restrictive: "[A]ny claim fails to respect reciprocity if it imposes a requirement on other citizens to adopt one's sectarian way of life as a condition of gaining access to the moral understanding that is essential to judging the validity of one's moral claims."[9] Over the past two decades, a substantial debate has developed over the nature of what John Rawls calls "public reason."[10] It may well make sense to urge all citizens to do their best to translate their commitments into terms that can be understood by citizens who do not share them. But the norm of reciprocity should not be interpreted to screen out the kinds of core beliefs that give meaning and purpose to many lives. This caveat is especially important in the United States, where levels of religious belief and observance are far higher than in any other industrialized democracy. It is difficult to imagine that any liberal democracy can sustain conscientious support if it tells millions of its citizens that they cannot rightly say what they believe as part of democratic public dialogue.

I want to suggest that an inclusive understanding of public reason is especially appropriate in the context of what I have called defensive public claims. It is one thing to contend that the United States should be a "Christian nation" and should restore official Christian prayer to public schools. That was the situation that existed in the grade schools of my youth, when I (a Jew) was compelled to recite the

---

9 Ibid., p. 57.

10 The literature discussing Rawls's (evolving) proposal is already vast. For a good start, see Robert Audi and Nicholas Wolterstorff, *Religion in the Public Square* (Lanham, Md.: Rowman & Littlefield, 1997); Audi, *Religious Commitment and Secular Reason* (Cambridge: Cambridge University Press, 2000); Kent Greenawalt, *Private Consciences and Public Reasons* (New York: Oxford University Press, 1995); and Jeremy Waldron, "Religious Contributions in Public Deliberation," *San Diego Law Review* 30 (1993): 817–848.

Lord's Prayer. I do not see how such a regime could possibly be defended through legitimate public reasons. It is quite a different thing to seek, on conscientious grounds, defensive exemption from general public policies that may be legitimate and acceptable to a majority of citizens.

Suppose a fundamentalist parent said to a secular philosopher: "Because of the content of your deepest beliefs, you happen not to experience a conflict between those beliefs and the content of the public school curriculum. But if *you* believed what *I* believe, you would experience that conflict, and you would seek for your child what I am seeking for mine. Moreover, the accommodation I seek is one that I would readily grant, were our positions reversed. I am not asking you to enter into the perspective of my particular religious beliefs. But I am asking you to enlarge your sympathies by imagining what it would be like to be in my shoes."

This fundamentalist is offering, as a public reason, not the specific *content* of religious belief but, rather, the *fact* of that belief and of the resulting clash with secular public policies. The secular interlocutor is being asked to experience that clash imaginatively as part of a process that could create a wider shared understanding – even if the particulars of faith are not easily communicable. I do not see why such a request is outside the legitimate bounds of public reason.[11]

Gutmann and Thompson insist that "[t]here is a public interest in educating good citizens, and no citizen can fairly claim that what constitutes good citizenship is whatever happens to conform to his or her particular religion."[12] This proposition is true as far as it goes. But as applied to the clash between the fundamentalist parents and the public schools, it raises three issues that are specific instances of the broad questions with which this chapter begins.

11 Especially for Gutmann, who praises the cultivation of the imagination as an important (and politically relevant) goal of education ["Civic Education and Social Diversity," *Ethics* 105 (April 1995): 572]. She properly raises the question of how imaginative powers are to be strengthened. But it is hardly obvious that the answer must exclude religious texts and arguments. At our son's bar mitzvah, our rabbi commented that students' engagement with the lives of Jewish patriarchs and matriarchs – especially the portions of their lives that seem strangest to modern readers – can be a powerful force for the cultivation of imaginative sympathies. That was certainly true for our son, who wrestled productively (if not wholly successfully) with the question of why Sarah asked Abraham to have a child by Hagar, and why Abraham consented.

12 Gutmann and Thompson, *Democracy and Disagreement*, p. 67.

The first is empirical: Is it the case that the accommodation sought by the fundamentalist parents would significantly impair the development of democratic citizens? The Hawkins County School Board never offered evidence on this point, and it is hard to see how they could have done so. Besides, as we have seen, in the United States the right of parents to withdraw their children from the public schools and send them instead to private and parochial schools enjoys constitutional protection. It is hard to believe that the consequences of such a choice for democratic citizenship are more favorable than a policy of accommodation with the public schools would have been. (Perhaps Gutmann and Thompson believe that *Pierce v. Society of Sisters* was wrongly decided and that the logic of deliberative democracy requires that all children be sent to public schools. Or perhaps they believe, as Stephen Macedo does, that the sphere of legitimate state regulation of private schools is so wide as to obviate this problem.)[13]

The second issue raised by Gutmann and Thompson's assertion is conceptual: How is the good citizenship whose development we seek through education to be defined? The answer is contested, and in any event it is likely to be complex. The capacity for deliberation is surely one element, but there are others, such as law-abidingness, personal responsibility, and the willingness to do one's share (through taxes, jury duty, military service, etc.) to sustain a system of social cooperation. In comparing the civic consequences of different educational strategies, one must examine all relevant dimensions, not just one. It is possible that on average, the graduates of Christian academies are less well prepared for democratic deliberation than are graduates of the best public schools (I know of no evidence bearing on this one way or the other). Nonetheless, they may be better citizens in other respects.

The final issue cuts even deeper. Suppose it is the case that a particular public policy is conducive to the cultivation of democratic citizenship.

13 Macedo, "Liberal Civic Education and Religious Fundamentalism: The Case of God v. John Rawls?" *Ethics* 105 (April 1995): 486. I find it difficult to believe that the "exposure to diversity" Macedo believes is essential to the inculcation of liberal tolerance in children is likely to succeed if it is crammed down the throats of their parents. I believe that in the long run, the *practice* of toleration – the policy of providing the widest possible scope for diversity consistent with the minimum requirements of liberal social unity – offers the best hope of generating gratitude toward the regime that makes this possible and hence support for the principle of toleration itself.

Does it follow that this policy is always right or permissible? For liberal pluralists, the answer is no, not always. Expressive liberty and political pluralism serve to limit the state's power to mold individuals into citizens. That is what it means to affirm a sphere of parental power not subject to state control. And as we saw, that is the clear meaning of *Meyer v. Nebraska* and *Pierce v. Society of Sisters*. There is, as Gutmann and Thompson rightly insist, an important public interest in educating good citizens. But there are other morally significant interests with which the formation of citizens sometimes comes into conflict, and to which the claims of citizenship must sometimes give way.

A liberal pluralist society will organize itself around the principle of maximum feasible accommodation of diverse legitimate ways of life, limited only by the minimum requirements of civic unity. This principle expresses (and requires) the practice of tolerance – the conscientious reluctance to act in ways that impede others from living in accordance with their various conceptions of what gives life meaning and worth. Tolerance is the virtue sustaining the social practices and political institutions that make expressive liberty possible.

Gutmann and Thompson criticize this way of thinking on the grounds that it

would not go far enough for the purposes of deliberative democracy. It provides no positive basis on which citizens can expect to resolve their moral disagreements in the future. Citizens go their separate ways, keeping their moral reasons to themselves, avoiding moral engagement. This may sometimes keep the peace.... But *mere toleration* also locks into place the moral divisions in society and makes collective moral progress far more difficult.[14]

In my view, Gutmann and Thompson are far too optimistic about the actual possibilities of resolving moral disagreements, and much too grudging about the practical worth of toleration. In most times and places, the avoidance of repression and bloody conflict is in itself a morally significant achievement – all the more so if it is based on internalized norms of restraint, rather than on a modus vivendi reflecting a balance of power. The agreement to disagree is a way of dealing with moral disagreement that is not necessarily inferior to agreement on the

14 Gutmann and Thompson, *Democracy and Disagreement*, p. 62; emphasis added.

substance of the issue. In the real world, there is nothing "mere" about toleration. As Michael Walzer says,

Toleration itself is often underestimated, as if it is the least we can do for our fellows, the most minimal of their entitlements. In fact,...[e]ven the most grudging forms and precarious arrangements [of toleration] are very good things, sufficiently rare in human history that they require not only practical but also theoretical appreciation.[15]

I do not deny that "collective moral progress" is possible. But it is much rarer than one would like and (if history is any guide) at least as likely to be achieved through the exercise of political power, or military force, or slow unplanned processes of social abrasion and influence, as through democratic deliberation. Liberals have never scorned (indeed, they have rightly prized) principles of social organization that "lock into place" *religious* divisions in society. A society that makes room for a wide (though not unlimited) range of cultural and moral divisions is no less an achievement.

But to what extent is it possible to implement policies based on this principle? Wouldn't the kind of accommodation sought by the fundamentalist parents lead to a slippery slope of endless claims against public school systems, threatening to erode the essential conditions of civic unity? The actual sequence of events in Hawkins County suggests otherwise.

The parents raised objections not to the public school curriculum as a whole but to one specific line of English readers. They initially proposed to remove their children from reading classes every day and personally teach them out of different textbooks somewhere on the school grounds. The principal of the middle school rejected that proposal but said, "I can understand why you feel the way you do." He offered a counterproposal approved by the school superintendent and chairman of the school board: The children could go to the library during reading period, where they would read from an alternative textbook on their own, without parental involvement or supervision. The fundamentalist parents quickly accepted this offer and agreed on alternative readers. Within a few weeks, ten middle school children were using the readers.

If this accommodation had been accepted by all schools in Hawkins County, that would have been the end of the matter. But it was not. A

15 Michael Walzer, *On Toleration* (New Haven, Conn.: Yale University Press, 1997), p. xi.

number of elementary school principals refused to go along, and some children were suspended. The next month, after a contentious meeting, the school board changed course and suppressed the policy that had been implemented by the middle school with the approval of the board chairman. It was only at that juncture that the parents felt compelled to escalate a limited policy dispute into a broader legal controversy.[16]

In short, the parents were willing to play by the rules, enter into a civil dialogue with schools officials, and accept proposals that fell short of their original desires. The logic of their position was perfectly compatible with the principles of constitutional order and with a workable system of public education. There was no slippery slope.

This should not be surprising: The limited public education accommodation for the Old Order Amish endorsed by the Supreme Court in *Wisconsin v. Yoder*[17] a quarter of a century ago has not led to an escalation of faith-based demands. Indeed, few other groups have even sought similar treatment for themselves. Properly interpreted, a liberal pluralist constitution is capacious enough to accommodate groups whose beliefs and practices do not much resemble those of most college professors.

Still, accommodation cannot be unlimited; a constitution is not a suicide pact. A liberal pluralist order must have the capacity to articulate and defend its core principles, with coercive force if needed. I agree with Gutmann and Thompson that democracy cannot be understood simply as a set of procedures. The issue between us concerns the extent and substance of the principles that a democracy must enforce.

In my view (which I have discussed at length elsewhere), these principles include what is required for civil order, justice, and the basics of human development.[18] Beyond this limited uniformity, a liberal pluralist state insists on the importance of allowing human beings to live their lives in ways congruent with their varying conceptions of what gives life meaning and purpose. It is only on this basis – in theory and in practice – that a political community can embrace divergent views concerning the sources of authority and the content of good lives.

16 This history is drawn from Stephen Bates, *Battleground: One Mother's Crusade, The Religious Right, and the Struggle for Control of Our Classrooms* (New York: Poseidon, 1993), pp. 71–85.

17 406 U.S. 205 (1972).

18 Galston, *Justice and the Human Good* (Chicago: University of Chicago Press, 1980); and *Liberal Purposes: Goods, Virtues, and Diversity in the Liberal State* (Cambridge: Cambridge University Press, 1991).

For two millennia, political orders have grappled with the challenges posed by revealed religions that are not "civil" religions. Pluralist liberalism represents the most nearly adequate response to this challenge. At the heart of this conception of human society is a principled refusal to allow religion to engulf the political order, or politics to invade and dominate religion. Liberal pluralism reaches its full development when it extends this refusal to cover the widest possible range of moral and cultural difference as well.

PLURALIST LIBERTY AND THE RIGHT OF EXIT

This brings me to my concluding point. There are two models of free association. In the model favored by many liberals who place autonomy at the center of their morality and politics, freedom of association is subject to the constraint that the internal structure and practices of all groups must conform to the requirements of general public principles. I have already discussed the central difficulty with this requirement – its tendency toward intervention, homogenization, and the denial of genuine difference.

The liberal pluralist conception of associational freedom is very different. Within broad limits, civil associations may order their internal affairs as they see fit. Their norms and decision-making structures may significantly abridge individual freedom and autonomy without legitimating external state interference. But these associations may not coerce individuals to remain as members against their will, or create conditions that in practical terms make departure impossible.

The reason is this: It is possible to enjoy what I call expressive liberty within associations that are hierarchical and directive, so long as there is a reasonable fit between institutional structures and individual beliefs. But when the two diverge, continued membership is no longer compatible with expressive liberty, and coerced membership is a denial of expressive liberty. In circumstances of meaningful social pluralism, individual freedom is adequately protected by secure rights of exit, coupled with the existence of a wider society open to individuals wishing to leave their groups of origin.

This is in many respects an attractively straightforward view, but I am compelled to say that it is hardly unproblematic. There are, to begin with, entrance problems, for example, the fact that we are born into certain groups to which we do not choose to belong – an experience that can be restrictive as well as empowering and that in any event does not conform to the classic model of voluntary association. Perhaps more importantly, there are exit problems, especially if "exit" is understood substantively as well as formally. A meaningful right would seem to include at least the following elements: *knowledge conditions* – the awareness of alternatives to the life one is in fact living; *capacity conditions* – the ability to assess these alternatives if it comes to seem desirable to do so; *psychological conditions* – in particular, freedom from the kinds of brainwashing that give rise to heartrending deprogramming efforts of parents on behalf of their children, and more broadly, forms of coercion other than the purely physical that may give rise to warranted state interference on behalf of affected individuals; and finally, *fitness conditions* – the ability of exit-desiring individuals to participate effectively in at least some ways of life other than the ones they wish to leave. The pluralist concept of liberty is not just a philosophical abstraction; it is anchored in a concrete vision of a pluralist society in which different modes of individual and group flourishing have found a respected place and are available to individuals who for whatever reason have ceased to identify with their own way of life.

In short, while liberal pluralism rejects state promotion of individual autonomy as an intrinsic good, there is a form of liberty that is a higher-order liberal pluralist political good: namely, individuals' right of exit from groups and associations that make up civil society. Securing this liberty will require affirmative state protections against oppression carried out by groups against their members.

10

LIBERAL PLURALISM AND CIVIC GOODS

REASONABLE DOUBTS ABOUT LIBERAL PLURALISM

My account of liberal pluralism is bound to trouble many readers. If I am right, the consequences of value pluralism include the recognition that there are normatively grounded restraints on the right of the state to enforce conceptions of justice and good lives on families and voluntary associations, even when those conceptions are attractive and endorsed by a strong majority of citizens. It is understandable that many contemporary liberals find this aspect of liberal pluralism deeply disturbing. By limiting the power of public institutions to shape individual and group practices, it permits what these liberals regard as retrograde behavior based on benighted beliefs.[1] In many cases their judgment on the merits of these lives may well be correct. But if liberal pluralism means anything, it means internalized norms and habits that restrain us from compelling others to live life our way rather than theirs, even when we have good reason to believe that their way is mistaken.

Another key worry about liberal pluralism focuses on issues of power and public order. My account of political pluralism – of multiple sources of legitimate power – may seem to yield a dangerous indeterminacy when these diverse powers come into conflict. A key structural implication of pluralism is likely to intensify these doubts: Although some public disputes are unavoidable because they involve issues on which the political community as a whole cannot but take a stand, or which the community can only address through a system of uniform rules, many other disputes do not involve such issues. Liberal pluralist constitutionalism

---

1 For a book-length exposition of such a view, see Brian Barry, *Culture and Equality* (Cambridge, Mass.: Harvard University Press, 2001).

responds to this distinction by removing as many contested issues as possible from the sphere of national legislation or regulation, through a federalist strategy that geographically disperses public power.

WHY LIBERAL PLURALISM CAN PURSUE CIVIC GOODS

In light of these and related doubts, one may well wonder whether liberal pluralism constitutes a form of political association capable of avoiding anarchy, pursuing shared purposes, and forging an even minimally adequate common life among its citizens. The response focuses on three features of liberal pluralism: the implications of its institutional form; the requisites of citizenship; and the implications for justice.

Liberal Pluralism as a Regime

Liberal pluralism may be a chastened and restrained form of politics, but it is nonetheless a political regime with corresponding powers and requisites. Let me underscore what I argued in Chapter 1: To create a secure space within which individuals and groups may lead their lives in accordance with their diverse understandings of what gives life meaning and value, public institutions are needed. In working to secure this social space, liberal pluralist public institutions must often act in ways that restrict the activities of individuals and groups. From the standpoint of liberal pluralism, four kinds of considerations serve to justify such restrictions: first, solving coordination problems among legitimate activities and adjudicating unavoidable conflicts among them; second, deterring and when necessary punishing transgressions individuals may commit against one another; third, safeguarding the boundary separating legitimate from illegitimate variations among ways of life; and finally, securing the conditions – including the cultural and civic conditions – needed to sustain liberal pluralist institutions over time.

In the language of American constitutional jurisprudence, these four sets of conditions represent the "compelling state interests" that may suffice, at least in principle, to moderate or even override claims based on what I call expressive liberty, beginning but not ending with religion. Because the liberal pluralist state is committed to regarding many of the activities it feels compelled to restrict as valuable in their own right, the state will act cautiously, employing the narrowest means consistent with the attainment of compelling public ends.

Liberal Pluralist Citizenship

Because liberal pluralist institutions are not self-sustaining, the state may legitimately require civic education. Liberal pluralism is not a suicide pact; liberal pluralist institutions are not debarred from securing the conditions of their own perpetuation. The issue between liberal pluralists and liberals who reject pluralism is not the appropriateness of civic education per se but, rather, its necessary and permissible content. Liberal pluralists see civic education as instrumentally valuable for securing political goods, which do not exhaust the range of fundamental values. Civic education conducted in a liberal pluralist spirit will be robust but carefully restricted to essentials. Clashes with faith and conscience cannot be avoided, but they can be minimized.

One thing above all is clear: In practice, a likely result of liberal pluralist institutions will be a high degree of social diversity, which makes necessary the virtue of tolerance as a core attribute of liberal pluralist citizenship. This type of tolerance does not mean wishy-washiness or the propensity to doubt one's own position, the sort of thing Robert Frost had in mind when he defined a liberal as someone who cannot take his own side in an argument. It does not require an easy relativism about the good. It is compatible with engaged moral criticism of those with whom one differs. Toleration means, rather, a principled refusal to use coercive state power to impose one's own views on others, and therefore a commitment to moral competition through recruitment and persuasion alone.

Civic virtues are not innate. Liberal pluralism requires a parsimonious but vigorous system of civic education that teaches tolerance, so understood, and helps equip individuals with the virtues and competences they will need to perform as members of a liberal pluralist economy, society, and polity.[2]

---

2 I am inclined to believe that the account of these civic virtues I offered a decade ago in *Liberal Purposes* (Cambridge: Cambridge University Press, 1991), Chapter 10, remains serviceable within the liberal pluralist frame. Because each individual virtue raises its own specific questions, many of them complexly empirical, I am open to the possibility that the understanding of liberal pluralist civic virtue may need to be revised.

It is hard to believe that tolerance, so understood, can be cultivated without at least minimal awareness of the existence and nature of ways of life other than those of one's family and community. The state may establish educational guidelines pursuant to this compelling interest. What it may not do is prescribe curricula or pedagogic practices that aim to make students skeptical or critical of their own ways of life.

The challenge here is to hew a principled path between intrusion and laissez-faire. It is true, as Chandran Kukathas has argued, that minority cultural communities need not be integrated into the mainstream of modern society and that they may be in many respects quite illiberal. But it is not true without further ado that (as Kukathas goes on to argue), "[t]he wider society has no right to require particular standards or systems of education within such cultural groups or to force their schools to promote the dominant culture."[3] The liberal pluralist state has a legitimate and compelling interest in ensuring that the convictions, competences, and virtues required for liberal citizenship are widely shared. And thus, Kukathas's effort to defend gypsies against all requirements of formal education for their children cannot be sustained.

The stress on shared citizenship as the basis of public norms enforceable against groups raises the possibility of some intermediate status – analogous to that of resident aliens – for groups that are willing to abide by the basic laws of the community without making full claims upon it, in return for which they might be exempted from some of the requirements of full citizenship. John Rawls is surely right to suggest that a legitimate public order is a form of social cooperation and that all who participate in its benefits must bear their fair share of the burdens. To claim full citizenship in a liberal pluralist state is to accept a range of duties that may limit the expression of other values and attainment of other goods.

But precisely because citizen duties may entail sacrifices of value that weigh more heavily on some individuals and groups than on others, liberal pluralists are open to the possibility that the polity may offer its inhabitants a range of possibilities short of full citizenship. Law could define packages of reduced benefits, each with appropriately reduced burdens. The state would insist on certain essentials – such as obedience to criminal law and the conditions for exit rights – and offer basic

---

3 Chandran Kukathas, "Are There Any Cultural Rights?" *Political Theory* 20 (1992): 117.

protections. But individuals who did not wish to be regarded, for example, as citizens with full and equal rights to participate in collective decision making might be relieved of otherwise binding civic responsibilities, such as jury duty. Jeff Spinner-Halev offers an account of "partial citizenship" for members of groups that wish to withdraw substantially from the civic community in order to live out a distinctive vision of the good life shared by few others.[4] Lucas Swaine goes even farther, suggesting what he calls "semisovereign status"[5] for some of these groups.

All these forms of exit from full liberal pluralist citizenship are subject to some basic limits. Of course the liberal pluralist state could not allow withdrawing groups to practice slavery or human sacrifice. But it is not clear that a liberal pluralist state would fall under an equally stringent requirement to forbid withdrawing groups from practicing polygamy. (Writing from a perspective different from mine, but broadly pluralist, Martha Nussbaum reaches a similar conclusion.)[6]

Justice in the Liberal Pluralist State

It is reasonable as well as traditional to maintain that the citizens of a well-ordered political association share a conception of justice. If liberal pluralism ruled out such a conception, it would yield, at best, a form of association in which individuals and groups were linked by a modus vivendi vulnerable to shifting definitions of self-interest and balances of power.

Fortunately, liberal pluralism does not undermine the possibility of a shared understanding of justice. It leads instead to a partially determinate conception that allows for considerable variation reflecting cultural distinctiveness, political decision making, and the particular circumstances in which a community may find itself.

A basic element of the liberal pluralist conception of justice is the rule of law. Given the diversity of moral and religious understandings that is

4 Jeff Spinner-Halev, "Cultural Pluralism and Partial Citizenship," in Christian Joppke and Steven Lukes, eds., *Multicultural Questions* (Oxford: Oxford University Press, 1999), pp. 65–86.

5 Lucas Swaine, "How Ought Liberal Democracies to Treat Theocratic Communities?" *Ethics* III, 2: 302–343.

6 Martha Nussbaum, "Religion and Women's Equality: The Case of India," in Nancy Rosenblum, ed., *Obligations of Citizenship and Demands of Faith* (Princeton, N.J.: Princeton University Press, 2000), p. 375.

likely to characterize a liberal pluralist society, informal accommodation will not suffice to adjudicate differences. Liberal pluralist citizens will see law as limited but as authoritative within its legitimate sphere.

A second element is that liberal pluralists regard shared citizenship as a zone of equality. There is no basis for distinguishing among individuals who accept the full range of civic burdens as well as benefits and who are capable of discharging the essential duties of citizenship. That is, there is no basis for asymmetrical allocations of basic civic powers in which some normal adult citizens may speak, vote, organize, serve on juries, or participate in national defense but others may not. Nor is there any basis for the unequal enjoyment of civic rights, such as the protection of the law. This is not to say that every liberal pluralist community is required to specify the content of civic powers and rights in the same manner. It is to say that when the community does establish the content of rights and powers, it stands under the obligation to extend them to all citizens in full standing. (As we have seen, liberal pluralists are open to the possibility of accommodating within the political association those groups whose members may prefer to be something other than citizens in full standing.)

Third, experience suggests that public dialogue regarding distributive justice will revolve around the categories of equality, need, desert, and choice.[7] What a political community counts as a *need* will reflect not only the permanent conditions of human life and flourishing but also the community's specific economic and social circumstances. Liberal pluralists are committed, at a minimum, to a conception of need that allows individuals to ward off the great evils of the human condition. In unfortunate circumstances, political communities may not be able to meet these needs, even with great effort. But they must do their best.

From the public standpoint, what counts as *desert* will be relative to the specific public purposes to which individual political communities give priority at particular moments in their history. During times of war or emergency, for example, it is likely that communities will regard participation in defense and security-related activities as meriting special compensation. (Considerations of this sort contributed to the adoption

---

7 For a fuller discussion, see my *Liberal Purposes*, Chapters 8 and 9. Another useful discussion of these matters from a broadly pluralist point of view is David Miller's *Principles of Social Justice* (Cambridge, Mass.: Harvard University Press, 1999).

of the GI Bill in the United States after World War II.) At other times, individual communities will identify particular activities or occupations as making especially important contributions to the general welfare and will arrange systems of public compensation accordingly.

Every community builds an element of economic choice or exchange into its understanding of distributive justice, and every community embeds choice within publicly defined limits. Experience suggests that some restrictions on choice are so extreme as to undermine the possibility of generating wealth and satisfying legitimate preferences, while some exercises of choice may make it impossible to achieve valid public purposes. Within these broad limits, communities may decide for themselves the protections of (and restrictions on) economic choice that appear most compatible with maintaining equal citizenship and promoting shared purposes.

Finally, communities must decide how to define the claims of equality, again within broad limits. From a liberal pluralist standpoint, members of the community must enjoy an equal social minimum that allows them to meet basic needs and participate in the activities of citizenship. For those members who are capable of making a contribution to the community, honoring the principle of equality takes the form of ensuring fair access to the positions that enable individuals to contribute and receive compensation. For those who cannot, because of age or physical, mental, or emotional infirmity, the principle of equality requires alternative means for providing the social minimum.

Beyond this minimum, liberal pluralist polities may define for themselves the most appropriate balance between equality and inequality. Some may impose restrictions on permissible gaps between high and low wage earners; others may impose taxes on the accumulation of wealth and its intergenerational transmission. There is no general theory that obliges particular communities to resolve such matters in a uniform fashion; there is wide scope for legitimate variation, guided by public preferences articulated in public choices. Liberal pluralist justice shapes politics but cannot replace it.

WHY PLURALISM IS UNAVOIDABLE

Even if pluralist theory does its best, many will continue to long for a fuller kind of theory that lays down the law to politics – through strict lexical orderings among goods, through rights that function as universal trumps, and through homogeneous accounts of value that turn deliberation into calculation.

My response is simple: While we may want these more ambitious forms of theory, we cannot have them. The varieties of pluralism I have tried to describe and defend in this book are aspects of the moral universe we happen to inhabit. Pluralism is not a confession of philosophical incompleteness or incapacity; it is an assertion of philosophical truth.

Practical philosophy is (or ought to be) the theory of our practice. When we are trying to decide what to do, we are typically confronted with a multiplicity of worthy principles and genuine goods that are not neatly ordered and that cannot be translated into a common measure of value. This is not ignorance but, rather, the fact of the matter. That is why practical life is so hard. If we could reduce it to some form of quantitative calculation or resolve its quandaries by bowing to clearly dominant values, it would not be so hard. But we cannot, at least not without oversimplifying moral experience and running grave risks. In practice, in both our personal and our public lives, the pursuit of a single dominant value, whatever the cost, typically produces side consequences (in military parlance, collateral damage) that we ought not ignore and that few would willingly accept. To preserve our moral balance and our capacity for humane action, we must sometimes subordinate even the pursuit of justice to other weighty considerations.

It is perfectly true that acknowledging multiple sources of legitimate authority creates problems for political authority. Politics would be less fragile if its claims clearly took priority over the claims of kinship, of self-expression, of free thought, or of faith. Politics enjoys no such priority, and great evils ensue when the political order seeks to exercise it. Life would be simpler if there were clear rules to resolve the clashes between politics and its competitors. But there are not. When a parent, or artist, or faith community, or philosopher challenges the political system's right to constrain thought and action, those involved must seek ways of adjudicating the conflict that does not begin by begging the question and does not end in oppression.

Once more: Pluralism is not relativism. The distinction between good and evil is as objective as is the copresence of multiple competing goods.

A politics that does everything within reason to ward off or abolish the great evils of the human condition while allowing as much space as possible for the enactment of diverse but genuine human goods is probably the best we can hope for, or even imagine. In any event, it would represent a significant improvement for the vast majority of the human race.

INDEX